The Old Girls' Book of Spells

*the real meaning of
menopause, sex, car keys,
and other important stuff*

Cal Garrison

Red Wheel
Boston, MA / York Beach, ME

First published in 2002 by
Red Wheel/Weiser, LLC
York Beach, ME
With offices at:
368 Congress St.
Boston, MA 02210
www.redwheelweiser.com

Library of Congress Cataloging-in-Publication Data

Garrison, Cal.
  The old girls' book of spells : the real meaning of menopause, sex,
car keys & other important stuff / by Cal Garrison.
      p. cm.
   ISBN 1-59003-018-4 (alk. paper)
   1. Witchcraft. 2. Menopause–Miscellanea. 3. Middle aged
women–Miscellanea. I. Title.
   BF1572.M46 .G37 2002
   133.4'3'0846–dc21

                                        2002001040

Typeset in Kennerly
Printed in Canada

TCP

09 08 07 06 05 04 03 02
8 7 6 5 4 3 2 1

@ @ @

For my daughters Eliza, Julia, and Johanna.
Thanks for hanging in there and for always giving me
the benefit of the doubt.

CONTENTS

CHAPTER 1

The Real Meaning of Menopause & Other Important Stuff about Magic

Witchcraft, magic, and spell work are as old as time itself. There was a time, long before the Great Deluge, when the inhabitants of this planet had total control of their thought processes and could manifest anything just by thinking about it. But this "sixth sense," which was once as much a part of us as the other five, we now call "supernatural," simply because the mental pathway that accesses it has atrophied. Even though it appears as if we've lost that ability it is probably more accurate to say that it lies dormant. Somewhere in our collective unconscious, each one of us remembers how to awaken the sixth sense.

Our connection to our psychic abilities and our ability to tap our sixth sense actually strengthens as we become women of a certain age, or crones. Up until puberty the pineal gland, the gland that houses the third eye, is open and clear. Around the time we get our periods a shield of calcium forms around this gland. I'm not sure why, but I think it has something to do with needing all the higher vibrational energy to mate, conceive, and reproduce. This calcium shield stays in place until menopause, but at menopause it dissolves and the third eye is free to function without obstruction again.

All the freaking out that goes with having your period stop, all the emotional ups and downs, are really about the adjustment we make as these higher sensory perceptions reawaken. Even hot flashes are an expression of vital kundalini energy; they tell us to take all that heat and send it up to the third eye.

If it seems ridiculous to you that anyone would think about writing a book of spells expressly for crones, it should seem more ridiculous that it hasn't been done before. In the ancient Egyptian spiritual traditions women were not even considered to be ready for initiation until the age of forty-five. At that point, if a woman was chosen as a candidate for the priestess path, she had to spend the next twelve years in the temples of initiation that lined the Nile. Do the math. It took them till the age of fifty-seven to get to a place in themselves where their wisdom amounted to anything. Why we live in a culture that diminishes the power of the "elder" female is a question that is buried under mountains of patriarchal manipulation. The Egyptians must have known something about menopausal forces that we've certainly lost touch with. Here we are pumping hormones and whining about hot flashes when we could be connecting with the God head!

Menopause is a portal that takes us to higher levels of awareness. Younger women have it all going on in the "T & A" department, but their psychic intuitive abilities are clouded by the fact that 90 percent of that energy is going into their sexual-reproductive functions. After menopause, that force can't come forth reproductively anymore, but it doesn't disappear. But no one tells us that there's another purpose for that energy, so we accept it as a nuisance and take hormones to suppress it. In this book we'll be looking at using it to feed the higher spiritual centers instead.

There's a reason why all the old etchings and engravings of witches and their "doings" portray images of women with a lot of chin hairs whose bodies aren't exactly *Playboy* material. As crones, we have "the gift," girls! Maybe now that the veil is being lifted on all the secrets, the one that's kept menopausal women relegated to the junk bin will get blown away too.

A lot of what's in the book is spells—all kinds of spells that are particularly appropriate to our time of life. Spells for reviving passion, spells for bringing you business or getting a better job, spells to clear bad vibes in your home, spells to help you find your car keys (or any other lost object), spells to help you sell your home, spells for protecting you while you travel, spells for voiding a traffic citation. Some people will think you're crazy when you start talking about spell work, but it's really not crazy at all. The images that many of us associate with witchcraft, magic, and spell work hark back to the days of the Inquisition; they're bogus. There's nothing spooky or hocus-pocus here to steer clear of. Doing a spell is a simple matter of focusing and directing your thoughts on something that you would like to make happen in your life. It's an excellent way to direct wayward thoughts toward a constructive goal.

It's easier for most people to swallow the idea of "the power of positive thinking" than it is to consider "doing a spell" because it doesn't offend our puritanical programming. I am pretty sure Norman Vincent Peale was no fan of "The Great Beast." Nor am I. Even though there are plenty of people that worship Satan and practice the black arts, I am not concerned with these things in any way, shape, or form. At its essence, there's absolutely no difference between doing a spell and using positive thinking.

HOW DID I GET HERE?

My first experience with the enormous power of focused intentions happened when I was about ten years old. I was sitting in the back of the station wagon and my thirteen-year-old sister, Christine, was up front with her best friend Marcia. The two of them were making fun of me, and I was enraged at being humiliated and rejected. Christine and I had "issues" that dated back to her attempt to poison me when I was six. She had always had it in for me, and I never knew why. Whatever my feelings were toward her on that day, they must have reached critical mass. I wanted to retaliate, but all I could find in the back of the car was a common pin and a pointed Dixie cup. I fashioned a missile by sticking the pin through the point of the cup. Fueled with the force of my clear intention I aimed this little rocket at Christine and it flew right up her left nostril. I couldn't believe it but at the same time I wasn't the least bit surprised because that's exactly where I wanted it to go.

As I got older the witchy thing was something I adopted as a look. When I was in high school you had to dress preppy to be in. I looked too much like a sexually ambiguous gym teacher in those waspy outfits to get any attention from the boys. Thank God the Beatles came along and brought the "mod" look with them. I caked on the eyeliner and loaded up with black stockings and little pointy-toed black shoes. I traded my John Meyer of Norwich clothes for Edwardian frocks designed by Mary Quant. I turned myself into a little teen witch and got a huge amount of mileage out of being different. The deeper meanings of needing to look this way got lost behind clouds of marijuana smoke. But by the time I was eighteen, I was reading Tarot cards, and by the time I was twenty-three, I was doing spells. I had no idea what any of this was but it came very naturally to me.

I had a very turbulent and changeable love life when I was young and all of the magic I did centered on attracting love. When I was alone, I'd sit for hours and focus my mind on the person I was enamored with until I could see them in my inner vision. When their image was clear I would speak to them as if they were there with me, tell them how I felt, and mentally invite them to respond. Sometimes they materialized immediately. Sometimes I would get someone other than the person I was focusing on, but something always happened.

As I got more comfortable with what I was doing, I made small figures out of red wax to symbolize the object of my affection. I carved their names into the wax, wrapped these little "poppets" in red silk or felt, lit a candle, and spoke my intentions out loud. Later on I began anointing the wax figures with oils and writing down on paper whatever it was that I wanted to happen. These slips of paper were burned, buried, or carried with me, along with the little wax effigies. I want to repeat here that I didn't know what I was doing. I didn't read books on the subject because as far as I knew there were none. All of this came naturally. In some part of my self, spell work was something I just *knew* how to do.

During this time I was living in the country and spent a lot of time walking through the fields and woodlands. As I walked, I noticed the plants growing in the area. I *knew* somewhere inside myself that they were good for something, so I'd dig them up, take them home, and identify them using a stockpile of books on herbalism that I rooted out of my grandmother-in-law's bookcase. Pretty soon my house began to look like a tobacco barn, with dried herbs and weeds hanging everywhere. Trusting souls came to me when they were sick and walked away with teas, tinctures, and salves for whatever ailed them.

My knowledge of healing came from applying everything I read through trial and error. I read somewhere that mullein leaves soaked in oil for a month cured earaches. My oldest daughter was one of those babies that had a ton of earaches, so she was my first guinea pig. A few drops of warm mullein oil in Eliza's little ears saved me so many sleepless nights walking the floor with her, not to mention what it would have cost me to buy antibiotics. I learned that burdock roots boiled into a tea purified the blood, so I tried it and it made me feel like "Superwoman". I read that yarrow leaves stopped bleeding, so I used them every time I had a nosebleed and found them very effective. I had a surefire cure for poison ivy that I made out of Solomon's Seal root. When I discovered that these herbs had magical properties as well, I began incorporating them into my spell work.

Somewhere along the line someone passed a booklet on to me that drew connections between everything that grew in the wild and the planets that ruled them. Any herb, flower, root, bark, or seed vibrates at a specific frequency. These frequencies resonate with corresponding planetary vibrations. Plants that have an affinity with Venus are useful in love spells because by the Law of Similars, or the Hermetic Axiom, they have the capacity to attract the Venusian influence. Any plant that is ruled by Mars will draw support from that planet for spells that are meant to enhance courage, strength, and physical passion.

I also began studying astrology in 1964. My father, who wasn't into any of these things but *was* open minded enough to understand that I was a little "different," went out and bought me my first astrology book as a Christmas gift. I was sixteen. Over the next six years I devoured every book I could find on the subject and, by a stroke of good luck, ended up living one town away from a world famous astrologer. When he offered to teach classes at his home, I was there with bells on. Looking back, it amazes me that I had no sense that all of these interests were weaving themselves together in my life. Aside from the fact that the astrology lessons formed the basis for my career as a professional astrologer, what I learned about the stars made it possible for me to incorporate knowledge of the lunar cycles and planetary affinities into my spell work.

It wasn't until I was forty that I discovered that what had come naturally to me had a name, Wicca. Wicca as we know it today is the surviving remnant of the female druidic teachings. By that time my life had taken so many twists and turns there were a million reasons that I needed spell work! My mid-life crisis uprooted me completely and I ended up out in the boon-docks with a wild and crazy ex-Marine. Our plans to build a self-sufficient lifestyle got blown out of the water when he went on a hell of a bender. My kids looked at me one day and said, "Ma, we gotta get outta here!" So, we loaded up the Jimmy and split.

We ended up on welfare and times were pretty tough. It was then that the whole concept of practical magic really began to kick in. When I wasn't looking for work, I was casting circles and doing spells like a maniac. Through some sort of feminine magnetism, this magic drew a group of great women into my life. They were all into Wicca too. We started doing circles at the New and Full Moons, and at the equinoxes and the solstices, performing rituals to attract success, abundance, love, health, and anything else we needed. We used Wicca because we had no other way to help ourselves. We used our circle work to bring about changes that we were hard pressed to make any other way.

We never became strict about our rituals. We didn't go in for initiations, great rites, or formal hierarchal structures. We prac-ticed together when we felt like it and alone when it seemed more appropriate. Our magic was more akin to what the peasant women on the heaths and moors of the British Isles must have practiced way back when, whenever they were in need of something.

It's important to remember that the need to cast a spell is based in desires that are plain and simple. Sophisticated, arcane, elaborate rituals are unnecessary. Special knowledge helps, but it's far better to be connected to the wish with your heart and mind than it is to be an expert at repeating by rote someone else's words.

There is definitely an art to doing any type of spell work, but it comes from practice and experience and is totally an individual thing. As you acquire more experience you eventually learn what works and what doesn't. Keeping a record of what you do can help. The old books refer to this type of journal as "A Book of Shadows," but you can call it whatever you want. The point is, if you make things too complicated you'll be too intimidated to go ahead and just do it, so don't drive yourself crazy thinking that you're not ready or don't know enough. If you want to start doing spells, do it. Spell work is a natural thing and it will open doors that will take you to a million other places.

A warning: Before I go into more detail there is one thing I want you to remember. When you do this type of work you must keep in mind that only what is of the light, and only what is in the highest good for all concerned can be focused upon. If you are in love with someone, for instance, and they are already involved, it is in no one's highest good to work a spell to attract them. I have seen terrible results come to people who do this type of thing. Neither can you wish harm upon anyone or try in any way to over-turn conditions in someone else's life in order to further the conditions in your own. There is a reason for this and it is best summed up in what is known as "The Wiccan Rede."

> Bide the Wiccan law ye must,
> In perfect love, in perfect trust.
> Eight words the Wiccan rede fulfill;
> An ye harm none, do as ye will.
> And ever mind the rule of three:
> What ye send out, comes back to thee.

Follow this with mind and heart,
And merry ye meet, and merry ye part.

This is another way of saying "what goes around comes around." And believe me when I tell you, it does. We Wiccans say that anything you put out into the universe will come back to you three times. If your intentions have any form of negativity attached to them, you need to understand that you will receive back in triplicate whatever you send out. With that in mind, let's move on, and I'll share with you what I've learned.

CHAPTER 2

Preparation: Picking the Time, Purification, Paraphernalia

I said we'd keep things simple, but let's face it, there's a difference between doing a spell and brushing your teeth! It's always important to prepare yourself to do spell work.

TIMING. Certain spells are said to work best at particular phases of the moon or on specific days of the week. If you're doing work that involves attracting something to you, for example, it's best to do your spell between the New and the Full Moon. When the Moon is waxing, energy is building and this force is so magnetic it causes whatever we wish for to come straight to us. The druids taught that the sixth day after the New Moon was the most potent time to attract positive influences into your life.

If you're focusing on banishing influences that are blocking you in some way, then you'll want to pick a time during the two-week period where the Moon is waning. As the Moon passes fullness, it starts to shrink. Any spell you cast at this time will be affected by influences that cause problems to get smaller, be released, or disappear.

The following list will help you choose the most appropriate day for any given spell, but let me add that while picking the right day helps, most of us are too busy to be bothered, and any day will do in a pinch.

Monday/Moon	Emotional issues, children, birthing, growth, security, the mother, the family, or the home.
Tuesday/Mars	Guts, self-assertion, physical strength, or raw sexual energy.
Wednesday/Mercury	Communication, travel, paper signing, or learning. Remember, Mercury is Quicksilver—it moves quickly. Your spells will manifest much faster if you work on a Wednesday.
Thursday/Jupiter	Wealth, luck, and good fortune. Jupiter is a "legal" planet too, so if you're going to court, use Thursdays for your "litigious" spells.
Friday/Venus	L-O-V-E! Always do your love spells on Fridays when the Moon is waxing. Unless you're trying to dump someone, in which case you'd work on a Saturday.
Saturday/Saturn	Limiting, binding, and banishing. I use Saturdays to release unwanted people, banish unwanted problems, and make things go away.
Sunday/Sun	Light, success, confidence, and recognition. Since the Sun represents the life force, Sundays are especially good for healing spells.

PLACE. Once you've chosen the day, you'll need to set aside an hour or two for your work and find a place where you won't be disturbed. If you're working indoors, lock the door, unplug the phone, and draw the drapes. If you're working outdoors, then you'll have a host of other considerations that we'll discuss as we go along. Indoors or out, you'll need to pick a spot that allows you enough room to move around.

When you've established where you're going to work, clear away the clutter and make a mental note of where North, South, East, and West are. You can set up an altar in the center of your space, but it's not necessary. Altars give you a place to put things, but you can go crazy setting up an altar by someone else's prescribed rules. I don't dispute the reasons for the prescriptions, but I also don't think it matters much.

A lot of old magical principles got injected with a heavy dose of patriarchal, ritualistic, male energy when they got brought back out into the open in the early part of the twentieth century. It seems ridiculous to impose a lot of strict rules and controls on a tradition that has its roots in the feminine principle. The feminine way is not defined, so whatever way you set it up will work for you. The only rule I go by is this: If you decide to have an altar, position it so that you're facing North when you stand in front of it. But hey, feel free to break that rule, too, if you want to!

PURIFICATION. The next step involves purification. Since we all carry thoughts, feelings, and other people's vibrations around with us, it's important to eliminate as much of this energy as you can before you do your work. The best way to do this is to wash it away with a ritual bath or shower. Adding a cup of sea salt to your bath water or doing a sea salt rub while you shower are excellent ways to clear your energy field. Adding to your bath essential oils and herbs or flowers that resonate with the type of work you're doing is a great idea too, but if you're new at this it's more important to tune in to the fact that everything but your current intention is being washed away.

While you're cleansing yourself, try to connect with the idea that what you're about to do is something special and that your reasons for doing it are unique because they represent a response to one of your deepest desires. If, for some reason, you don't have time for or can't go through this bathing process, don't let that stop you. Sometimes it's quicker to smudge yourself with a sage wand.

Sage clears everything. It's excellent for clearing the mind of unwanted thoughts so that your *real* wisdom can come through.

WHAT TO WEAR. Once you're cleansed, find something loose and comfortable to wear. It doesn't have to be fancy, but it could be something a little different than your ordinary clothing. Regular clothes are fine, too, really. I would imagine the peasant women back in the old days didn't worry too much about what they were wearing when they did this type of work. I've done plenty of spells in my work clothes.

Which brings me to the next point. Some people prefer to work in the nude. When you're naked, there is nothing to separate you from the forces and elements that you'll invoke to assist you. But if you decide to work outdoors there are obvious reasons why it might be inappropriate to do a spell in your birthday suit. It's no fun to be preoccupied wondering if your neighbors are getting an eyeful when what you really want is to concentrate on your spell. When you work naked you have to know absolutely that there's no one peeking at you from behind the bushes or through the keyhole.

Once your body is purified and ready, it's a good idea to purify yourself mentally and emotionally too. I meditate as a matter of course before a spell. It clears away all of the astral junk that the bath or shower didn't eliminate. Being totally centered is important. But if meditation isn't your thing, then just take a few minutes to breathe deeply and be in the moment.

PARAPHERNALIA. Every time you do a spell, you will think in advance about what you'll need in the way of paraphernalia. I suggest that you read through the whole book once before you start so you can go out and get the stuff you need. Candles (in a variety of colors), matches, incense, writing materials, various essential oils and herbs, water, and sea salt are essentials. You *must* have these on hand.

As you get more used to doing spell work, your paraphernalia will expand to include crystals, magnets, mirrors, lodestones, silk cords, bones, pouches, feathers, photographs, hair, and anything else your imagination conjures up to aid you in your work.

Here's what I recommend: A few days before you do your magic, as you formulate what you intend to focus on, make a list of what you'll be using. Gather all of these supplies and have them ready before you take your bath. I have a big old picnic basket that I keep stocked with all this stuff. The reason it's important to collect everything and have it close at hand is because once you're actually engaged in doing the spell, it breaks your concentration to have to run to the kitchen or back to the house to get this or that. Being organized allows you to stay focused.

CASTING THE CIRCLE. So you have the right day, you've found the right spot, you have all of your tools ready, and you're clean as a whistle. What next? Keep in mind what I said earlier–spell work is easy, but not as easy as brushing your teeth. This is a special occasion and it's important to draw a line between what you're about to do and your other, more mundane activities. The first thing you're going to need is that bag of sea salt to cast a circle. I always cast a circle of salt around the area I'll be working in because sea salt forms a barrier of protection that nothing can penetrate except that which you invite in. Casting a circle with salt separates what will go on inside it from the energies of the outside world. Have a small pitcher or bowl of water ready.

I have a preference for beginning everything in the North. I am Swedish and have a whole lot of Viking in me, along with plenty of druid memories, so the North is home to me. Other traditions start at the East. You may feel more at ease using one of the other directions as your point of origin. From now on I will orient everything from the North, but you can start wherever it feels right to you.

Starting at the North point, move around the circle in a clockwise direction–North, East, South, West, and back to the North Point again. Clockwise is important. Counterclockwise movements are associated with the Devil and you don't want to do anything to call up that kind of energy. As you go you will sprinkle salt to mark the circle.

Now go get your pitcher or bowl of water, take it to the North Point and walk around the circle in a clockwise direction, sprinkling water over the salt. This seals the circle.

Next you will light your candle and walk around the circle once more. When you arrive back at the North point, go get your incense, light it with the candle, and take it around again, always moving clockwise.

The sea salt represents the Earth element, the water represents the Water element, the candle represents the Fire element, and the incense is symbolic of the Air element. On this plane the four elements–Earth, Water, Fire, and Air–are what make up the physical universe. By carrying each of the elements around the circle you are symbolically building your own smaller "universe" within the circle. Inside this space you are the sole creator, you are God, and whatever you want to make happen will happen. This is because the fifth element is Spirit and it is your Spirit, working with and through the other four elements that allows you to create and bring anything you want to fruition. That is the essence of magic. The five-pointed star, or pentagram, is the universal symbol for all good witches. It represents the four elements united and controlled by the fifth element of Spirit. The more connected you are to your own Spirit, or to your Higher Self, the more power you will have to be successful with your spell work.

CHARGING THE CIRCLE. The circle is cast, the candle is burning, the incense is filling the air around you. A few more things need to happen before you can get down to business. At this point, I like to stand in the center of the circle with my right arm extended and my forefinger pointed and twirl three times clockwise, envisioning a blue-violet flame coming out of my fingertip. This charges the circle. Sometimes you can actually see the space around you light up when you do this, but don't worry if that doesn't happen. If you feel silly doing this, skip it, but the next step is important.

CALLING IN THE GUARDIANS. There are "Guardians" who watch over the four corners of the universe. Their energy is extremely important and helpful to say the least. In the next phase of preparation, you are going to invite them to join you and assist you in your work. I go to the North, East, South, and West, respectively, and say the following:

Guardians of the watchtower of the North,
Element of Earth,
And all of thee in the realm of the bear,
I invite you to witness this rite,
And to protect this sacred space.

Guardians of the watchtower of the East,
Element of Air,
And all of thee in the realm of the raven,
I invite you to witness this rite,
And to protect this sacred space.

Guardians of the watchtower of the South,
Element of Fire,
And all of thee in the realm of the dragon,
I invite you to witness this rite,
And to protect this sacred space.

Guardians of the watchtower of the West,
Element of Water,
And all of thee in the realm of the mermaid,
I invite you to witness this rite,
And to protect this sacred space.

As I say these words at each cross-quarter, I "draw" a pentagram in the air with my forefinger. This part of the work is awesome to me. The forces you're calling in are archetypal energies that exist on another level. They are very much part of everything that happens everywhere on the physical plane even though we can't see them with our eyes. Calling in the Guardians is a humbling experience and needs to be approached with a certain amount of reverence. If the word reverence is too religious for you, respect will do. There are a million ways to invoke these Spirits. Until you find your own, borrow other people's words. Any book on Wicca will provide you with ideas. I do it this way because it feels right to me.

CLOSING THE CIRCLE. Once your work in the circle is done, you can't leave these forces hanging around. Anything that's powerful enough to "invoke" can't be left twiddling their thumbs in your living room or yard! So when your spell is finished, go back to the North, East, South, and West points, thank each Guardian for its assistance, and send them back from whence they came. These are the words I use to send the Guardians home when I close my circles.

We thank you for coming to assist us in this work and bid you hail and farewell.

Guardians of the North (East, South, West), return to thy place. Leave peace to reign in time and space.

Once I've sent the Guardians home, I twirl around clockwise with my right arm extended and clear the circle. When the work is done, it's done. You can't leave circles hanging around all over the place. This doesn't erase the spell. It lifts the circle and frees the energy that was raised inside it to mingle with the collective unconscious.

READY TO ROLL. Now that you know where to start, you're ready to work. Every time you do a spell you will go through each of the steps we've discussed here. If all of this feels a little too "out there" for you, and you want to do your magic without the mumbo-jumbo, go ahead. Your spells may be more successful if you take the time to set the vibration up a few notches, but there are no rules that say one way is any better than any other. Ultimately, the only things that matter are your ability to focus your thoughts and the power of your intention. The proof will lie in whether your spells get the result you are aiming for.

CHAPTER 3

Relationship Spells: Making (or Breaking) Connections of All Kinds

We Old Girls know a thing or two about relationships. Chances are you've at least been in a few by now. And whether or not you're in a one-on-one thing, you still interact with your kids, parents (if they're still here), friends, coworkers, neighbors, and relatives. Even if you live in a cave on a Himalayan mountaintop, you have relationships–to nature, Earth, the sky, and the stars. There's just no getting around them.

If you're living with someone at this stage of the game, you have a particular set of issues to deal with. If you're still having fun together, all I can say is lucky you, but it's just as likely that you've become like ghosts who just happen to be haunting the same house. Or that you drive each other completely nuts and have accepted that. I don't know–maybe you don't even want to hear about relationships because you're getting it on with the UPS man/woman and it brings up too much guilt!

A lot of us Old Girls tell ourselves that we've "chosen" to live without a partner because it's easier. You bet you're a– it's easier, but "easier" implies that there are things about yourself that you just don't want to see. Relationships are mirrors and *all* our relationships show us who we are. When you close yourself off to them, you seal the entrance to the cave that leads to who you are.

The truth is, when you're working on your relationships, the one you have with yourself is the most important, so our first spell is one you can use to reconnect with *you*.

The "Hello, It's Me, Let's Reconnect" Spell

WHAT YOU'LL NEED

A mirror
An apple
A knife
A pink votive candle
Matches
Your favorite incense
A cup each of sea salt and Epsom salts
A pair of flannel PJ's or a flannel nightie.
An old T-shirt would work, too.
I also recommend playing some music that you love.

The New Moon is the best time to do this spell,
but any time you feel the need is the right time.
Allow yourself a good hour or more.

℮ ℮ ℮

Cast a circle if you wish. Light your candle and set your incense to burn. Take off all your clothes and stand or sit in front of the mirror. It's okay if you can't deal with being naked, but you're going to take a bath as part of this so you'll have to strip sooner or later.

Look at yourself in the mirror. Send love to all the parts of your body, including your internal organs. Tell yourself how much you love yourself and how much you've missed you. (The "inner critic" will be going full blast while you're doing this. Gently tell it to get lost.) Lock eyes with your eyes in the mirror. If you cross your eyes a little, the reflection in the mirror will show you one big eye. That big eye is your third eye and it goes straight to your soul.

As you look into your third eye, see what's in your soul and be open to receiving the love that the Spirit inside you feels for you. Love it back. Now slice the apple in half. Take one apple seed from each half and switch them. Now eat the half that sits to the left, seeds and all. Send that apple down into the core of your being and let it nourish your beautiful Spirit. Savor this fruit and save the other half for later.

When you feel complete, fill up the bathtub, adding your sea salt and Epsom salts. Get into the tub and close your eyes. Imagine you are back in your mother's womb, just be a baby. Love this new little baby. It's who you are. When the time is right, get out of the tub, go put on your PJ's, snuff out the candle, and curl up in bed. Fall asleep if you want to, you'll probably be pooped. When you wake up, you will be fully reconnected with your inner self. Get dressed, and go bury the other half of the apple in the ground, along with what's left of the candle. This will maintain your con-nection with yourself until the next New Moon, or for the next twenty-eight days.

SPELL TO STRENGTHEN YOUR CONNECTION TO YOUR PARTNER

This isn't what I'd call a "love" spell, exactly. It's something that I use when the feeling of spiritual connection between me and my lover needs a transfusion. Taking each other for granted is easy. When we fall asleep in our relationships, we often need some help waking up and remembering that the same beautiful something that brought us together with our partners is still there between us. When you get to the point where you want to reconnect with what that is, use this spell.

By the way, this spell can be used to strengthen the bond in any relationship that needs life blown into it. Don't feel limited to just your partner. Use it on your friends, your kids, your parents, your boss, or your coworkers. It goes with everything!

The "Let's Remember Why We're Together" Spell

<u>WHAT YOU'LL NEED</u>

2 pink candles
A nail
Rose oil or your favorite essential oil
Your favorite incense
Coffee grounds
String
Parchment or paper cut from a brown paper bag
A pen
Matches

The New Moon is the best time to do this spell, but if that's not convenient try to pick a Thursday, a Friday, or a Sunday.

ℰ ℰ ℰ

Cast a circle if you wish, and if you have an altar use it for this spell. Light the incense. With the nail, inscribe one candle with your name and one with your partner's name. Now anoint them from wick to base with the essential oil. When you anoint any candle with an essential oil you are turning up the volume on your work. Every oil resonates at the same frequency as the herbs and flowers that go into it. Oils are chosen for each spell because the flowers they are pressed from attract the influence of the planet whose support you are enlisting. The act of holding the candle in your hands and rubbing it with oil should be done with focus and intention. What would be just any other candle is now imbued with the essence of the oil itself and all the thought forms held in your mind. Because any oil acts as a carrier, the anointed candle carries the energy you're trying to attract or dispel along the length of the taper. The flame ignites it and all your wishes are intensified. When the spell involves attracting something into your life, anoint the candle from wick to base so the energy can come in. When you're trying to banish an influence, anoint the candle from the base to the wick so that those energies can depart.

When you have anointed both candles, roll each one in the coffee grounds and rub it all in so that the names you've inscribed show on the surface of the candle. Set both candles in front of you and light the one with your name on it. As you do this, know that this flame is your desire. As it burns, write down on your paper what it is you feel in your heart right now for you partner. You can write whatever you want, but try to focus on what it is you would like to have happen so that the two of you can feel connected again. Read it out loud and when you're done, set the paper face up underneath your partner's candle.

Now light the candle with your partner's name on it. Look into the flame and invoke his or her presence or essence. As you visualize this, tell him or her everything you want and everything that's in your heart. Let it all hang out!

The next part might seem a little tricky. Just try it. As you *feel* your partner's presence, listen and see if you can *hear* what he or she is telling you about what he or she needs and wants from the relationship right now.

Relax your eyes enough to see both candle flames become one. Stay in this place for as long as it takes for you to feel complete. Snuff out the candles. Wrap the paper you've written on around the base of both candles. Tie everything together with the string.

Once a day until the candles burn down, light them for a few moments and sit in front of them, focusing your mind and heart on what reconnecting with your lover really means to you.

When everything is burned down, bury it all in the ground or throw it into the nearest body of moving water. This spell will begin to get results immediately and should definitely manifest by the next New Moon or within twenty-eight days.

SPELL TO HEAL YOUR CONNECTION
TO YOUR MOTHER OR FATHER

No matter how wonderful you think your childhood was, how much you've been able to overlook, how much you love or hate your parents, your connection to them is the one that has you by the ovaries. Every parent-child relationship needs some healing. Whether your parents are living or long gone, you can still connect to them through this spell. Actually, sometimes I think it's easier to get your point across to them when they're dead because from that vantage point they listen better and can finally see what the score is.

Dealing with your issues on the etheric or spiritual level is more effective than trying to iron them out in person. You can have a conversation with anyone in spirit and it's much easier to communicate clearly because the personalities and the issues of the personalities aren't running the show. If you're someone who's had a tremendous amount of abuse from your parents for instance, talking to them in spirit is ten times easier than it would be if you had to confront them in person.

This spell is for those times when you need to make peace with Mom and Dad. It is especially useful when your parents are too sick or senile to hold a conversation.

The "Come In, Mom and Dad" Spell

WHAT YOU'LL NEED

A photograph of one or both parents
(if you don't have pictures of them,
two pieces of paper with their names on them is fine)
A white candle for Dad
A black candle for Mom
A blue candle for peace
A photograph of yourself
Your favorite incense
Dust from under the bed

A lock of your hair
A piece of blue cloth
String
Rose oil
A nail
Matches
A box of tissues (this one's a real tear jerker.
If you're a cryer, have your tissue ready.)

You'll need a waning moon for this one because you're releasing the past and letting go of the emotions that have prevented you from accepting the way things are.

ℰ ℰ ℰ

Use your altar and cast a circle if you wish. Set the incense to burn. Anoint the candles wick to base with the rose oil. With the nail, you can inscribe the words "I love you" or "I forgive you" or both, on each candle if you wish. On the left, place the black candle with the picture of your mother underneath it. On the right, place the white candle with the picture of your father underneath it. Put the picture of yourself underneath the blue candle and place it so that the three candles form a downward pointing triangle. Light the candles, starting with Mom, then Dad, then you. Put the lock of hair in the center of the triangle. Invoke the spiritual presence of your parents and say these words out loud:

I have loved you from the beginning
As you have both loved me.
At this moment as I conjure you,
Love is all that I can see.
All the tears within my heart
Have left and so has the pain.
I feel you know as I do that only love remains.

Stay in this moment long enough to feel the connection to what you're doing. When you're ready, wrap all three photographs, the lock of hair, and the dust from under the bed inside the blue cloth. Tie it with the string like a little pouch. (For those of you who haven't figured it out, the dust from under the bed is a symbol for what your issues with your parents amount to–nothing.)

Every day until the candles burn down, sit in front of them for a while or just let them burn as you go about your business. Keep the pouch and sleep with it under your pillow. When there's nothing left of the candles, burn the remains and the pouch in the metal bowl. What goes up in smoke will be carried up to the etheric level and go exactly where it needs to go.

SPELL TO USE WHEN THERE'S A ROLE REVERSAL IN THE PARENT-CHILD RELATIONSHIP

One of the things that often comes with our entrance into cronehood is the need to become a "parent" to one, or sometimes both of our parents. The point where we realize that that's what's happening requires us to shift far enough away from our own "stuff" to take it on. At first it's disconcerting, because we go along for years assuming that we will always be the child in those relationships. It's especially upsetting for those of us who've been running on the hope that just maybe, one day, Mom and Dad would turn around and finally be there for us. Life is a series of curveballs and this is one of them. For those of you who are battling with the need to switch roles with your parent(s), this spell will help you come to terms with the experience in your heart and in your mind.

The "It's My Turn to Take Care of You" Spell

WHAT YOU'LL NEED

A photograph of yourself as a child
A photograph of your mother or father as they are now

Scissors and tape
Parchment or paper cut from a brown paper bag
A pen
Your favorite incense
2 candles, you choose the colors
A nail
Rose or patchouli oil
An eggshell broken in half
A square piece of cloth cut from an old blanket
A piece of red cloth a little bigger than the blanket square
String
A metal bowl on a fireproof trivet and matches for burning

—————————————————————

It's best to do this just after the Full Moon. The waning cycle is optimal for anything that needs to be released.

ⓔ ⓔ ⓔ

Cast your circle and work with an altar if you want to. Light the incense. As it burns, inscribe "Mother and Father" on one of the candles and "Child" on the other one with the nail. Anoint both candles wick to base with the oil. Set them up in front of you with the picture of yourself under your candle and the picture of your parent(s) under their candle.

Call up the spiritual presence of your parent(s) and remember how things used to be. Whether it's bad or good makes no difference at this point. The idea is to get clear about how things were. When you feel complete about this, take the photographs from under each candle and lay them side by side. With your scissors, cut the faces out of each picture and tape your face over your parent's photo where their face used to be. Now tape their face(s) over the picture of you as a child. Think about how things are now, and with your pen and paper write down everything you are feeling about this role shift.

Rub three drops of oil into the paper, kiss it once, and cut it in half. Put one half under each candle. As you do this, put the photo that has your face on it under the parental candle. Put the photo that has your parent's face on it under the child candle. Sit for a few minutes with your eyes closed focused on the reality of how things are. When you have accepted this shift in your heart and soul, say these words out loud:

> *I've become you,*
> *And you've become me,*
> *Life turns us around*
> *And our hearts let it be.*

Now burn the picture with your parent's face on it in the metal bowl. When there's nothing left, put the ashes inside the eggshell and tape the eggshell together. Take the picture that has your face on it along with the note you wrote and wrap them around the eggshell. Now wrap all of this up inside the piece of blanket and place this charm on the red cloth. Tie the red cloth around everything to make a little pouch.

For the next few days (up to two weeks), keep the pouch under your mattress. Light your "parent-child" candles every day for a few minutes until they burn all the way down, then bury them in the ground or cast them into the nearest body of moving water, along with the pouch.

The Water element is the emotional element and this is an emotional spell. As you cast what's left of your candles into the water, you are returning the energy called up in the spell to the waters of life and the womb of creation. Something new will be reborn in those waters.

This whole process may call up a lot of intense feelings for you. If it does let go and express whatever's in your heart. I always find it helpful to lie face down on the ground and cry. Sometimes I even jump in the water and go for a swim. Your response will be your own so do whatever Spirit calls you to do.

SPELL TO STRENGTHEN THE
CORD THAT BONDS YOU TO YOUR KIDS

The relationships we have with our children also change over time. As they grow up, we have to let them go. At this point in our lives, most of our kids are grown and living on their own. Even if you're lucky enough to have your kids nearby, what goes on in their lives is none of your business. That's a hard one for a lot of us. Of course, we want things to work out for them, and as they experience their own adulthood and the choices that come with it, it's often hard to watch them learn from their mistakes. And when they don't learn from them, it's even harder. Too bad it's innappropriate to meddle, but it is. Besides, we have our own issues to wrestle with and are all tied up trying to get our own lives right! The best we can do is keep the love flowing.

This spell is a way to connect to your kids by remote. It keeps the flow of love from heart to heart wide open. It also protects them and ensures that Mother Earth will help them handle the things that they can't.

This spell works great for grandchildren, too.

The "I'm Always There In Your Heart" Spell

WHAT YOU'LL NEED

As many small stones as there are kids
Something to write on the stones with
Some string
A blue candle
Your favorite incense
A piece of blue cloth big enough to wrap the stones in
A piece of red cloth the same size
A thistle or an iron nail
Some sage
Rose oil

A lock of your hair (if you're going bald,
use a photograph of yourself!)
A small bowl filled with milk

You can do this spell *any* time, but Mondays
are best because the Moon rules Monday and children
are ruled by the Moon, too. If you want to be
politically correct, pick a night when the Moon's in Cancer
because Cancer is the sign of mother and child.

℮ ℮ ℮

Cast a circle and use your altar if you want to, and light the incense. Inscribe the candle with the names of all your children or the name of the child you are most concerned about. Anoint the candle wick to base with the rose oil and light it.

On the stones representing sons, draw the Teiwaz rune ↑. The runes are magical symbols and so ancient no one really knows where they came from. There are twenty-four of them (some people use twenty-five) and each one is a sacred symbol with a specific meaning etched on a piece of bone, wood, or stone. Runes are always carried in a pouch. Whenever I have a question, I reach into my rune bag and draw out a symbol to provide me with insight and clarity. I use runes a lot in my spell work because their great power and meaning help to amplify whatever I am doing.

On stones representing daughters, inscribe the Berkana rune ᛒ. As you do this, hold the feelings in your heart and the images of your children together in your inner vision.

Soak the string in the milk. When this is done, tie each stone with string like a little package and leave a tail of string about eight inches long hanging from each stone. Tie each piece of the excess string to the lock of hair. If you're using a photograph of yourself roll it into a scroll and tie the strings to that. Lay the piece of blue cloth in front of you. Place the charm you've just made on top of it. Sprinkle sage over everything and add the thistle or the iron nail.

Now take time to offer any prayer you wish up to the spirits that watch over your children, or say these words out loud:

> *You are always in my heart.*
> *My love surrounds you day and night.*
> *The moon and stars now take my part*
> *As you find your way back to the light.*

When you feel complete about this, wrap everything in the blue cloth and tie it with string to make a little pouch. The blue is for peace. Now wrap this pouch with the piece of red cloth and tie it with more string. The red is for protection. Hold the charm in your left hand and charge it with your love. When you are ready, snuff the candle.

Tie the pouch to your bedpost, keep it under your pillow, or carry it with you wherever you go. Bring the bowl of milk outside and pour it into the Earth. The Great Mother will take care of the rest. Light the candle every day for a little while until it burns out. When it's all gone, bury it where you poured the milk.

SPECIAL CHARM FOR A SWEET GRANDCHILD

You don't need to do any special spells for your grandchildren. They're so perfect that there's no need to mess with this perfection, but it is nice to surround them with love and protection. Here is a sweet little charm you can hang over the crib or on their bedpost.

This is also a great one to make whenever it's time to welcome any new Spirit into the world.

The "Grandma's Love Surrounds You" Charm

WHAT YOU'LL NEED

A piece of blue cloth
An iron nail

Any kind of dried bean
A small stone or a piece of rose quartz
A cinnamon stick or powdered cinnamon
Caraway seeds
Lavender oil
A bright piece of ribbon and some lace
Something to write on the stone with
A little note that says "I love you"

It makes absolutely no difference when you do this. You never know when little babies are going to come into the world so feel free to make this charm whenever the Spirit moves you.

℮ ℮ ℮

You can cast a circle and burn a little incense if you want to, but all that really matters here is that your heart be open and full of love. Lay all your ingredients out in front of you. One by one, charge the nail, the bean, the cinnamon, the caraway seeds, the love note, the ribbon, and the lace in your left hand with all the love you have. Place them on the cloth. Now charge the rose quartz in the same way. If you're making this for a boy, inscribe the stone with the Teiwaz rune ↑. If you're make the charm for a girl, inscribe the stone with the Berkana rune ᛒ.

Charge the stone in your left hand with the wish that this child be surrounded with protection day and night. Place the stones on the cloth with the other ingredients and the love note and sprinkle it all with three drops of lavender oil. Wrap everything in the cloth. Now wrap the lace around the cloth and tie it with the ribbon like a little sachet to hang over your grandchild's crib or bedpost (making sure to choose a safe spot, of course).

You're all set! This is a wonderful way to "be there" for your grandkids even when you're far away.

CHAPTER 4

Love (and Sex) in the Time of The Change

You could be completely jaded about love at this point. A lot of us are. I know just as many women who are die-hard romantics waiting for that fairy-tale to come true. Once in a while, I even come across women who have actually figured out how to maintain a healthy connection with another person. Whatever the story is, we're not different than our younger sisters when it comes to love. We just have more experience.

Isn't it ironic that by the time we've lived enough to have a vague idea of what love is, there's a general assumption that we're too old, it's too late, or why bother to pursue it? And who would want us anyway with the crow's feet, one breast, and thighs that don't know how to behave?

The reason we came to this planet is to learn what it means to give and receive love and to see God reflected in the eyes of another person. If you're anywhere near fifty or beyond and still think that love is floating out there as a possibility, I'm right there with you. I think it's more of a possibility than it was when we were younger.

There's a huge belief that we dry up sexually around menopause. If that's true for some people, it may have less to do with menopause and more to do with your relationship or to the way you've been relating to yourself sexually all along. I have heard people say that you lose your sex drive and your need to be sexual after you go through "The Change." I don't know about you, but I don't buy it. The concept of a "Second Spring" is alive and well, girls!

Sex is a portal to spiritual realms that are harder to reach prior to menopause. When you eliminate it from your life you are ripping yourself off. I'm no nymphomaniac, but I found that everything about sex became easier and less complicated after menopause. There are plenty of us out there who would agree.

So spells for love and spells for lust are just as important now as they were when we were twenty, probably more so. With your third eye wide open, you'll definitely get more mileage out of them.

Of course there are ethics as far as this stuff goes. You have to decide for yourself, I suppose, what's emotionally and spiritually "legal" in your universe. In my world, for instance, it's not okay to work a spell on someone who's already attached. Okay, maybe if they're not legally married, it's kosher, but that all depends on the situation. I've been with the same man for over twelve years and we're not married but we're very committed to each other. The fact that we've chosen not to honor the commitment legally is our business. I would be pretty pissed off if some "witchy-girl" was working overtime doing love spells to draw my sweetheart to her bed-side. There's definitely a "gray area" in the love spell department and the situation described above is a lot different than it would be if we were just a couple of people who dated once in a while.

Every set of circumstances is unique, and your decisions about who to pursue have to be made from your own place of integrity. Some people say it's not okay to project a specific set of intentions onto *anyone* because you're interfering with their free will. You could also be getting in your own way by fixating on someone specific. After all, none of us knows what our romantic destiny is.

I'm not sure how I feel about this. If you're attracted to some-one, I think it's fine to work a spell to draw them to you. If they don't materialize after a certain amount of time and effort, it's important to realize that you're probably barking up the wrong tree! Of course you can go overboard being politically correct with this stuff, just as you can with anything else. I've always been attracted to the women who practice Cajun or Creole voodoo.

They don't deny their darker emotions and have a no-holds-barred approach to spell work that is really wild. In their world, it's legal to do anything. My advice is to think through your ethical issues and make up your own mind.

CANDLE SPELL TO ATTRACT LOVE

The "Bring My Perfect Mate to Me" Spell

What you'll need

A pink or red candle (pink if you're trying to attract,
red for sex; use a votive or a pillar candle
depending on how much time you want to put into this)
A photograph of the person you wish to attract
1 or 2 pieces of parchment or
paper cut from a brown paper bag.
Any 1, or a mixture, of the following oils: rose, musk, patchouli,
strawberry, gardenia, vanilla, or clove
Orrisroot powder or ground cinnamon
A nail
Something to write with
A piece of pink cloth
String
Matches
A metal bowl and a fireproof trivet

The best time to work love spells is on a Friday while the moon is waxing. Venus rules Friday and you definitely want her on your team. Avoid Saturdays, unless you're trying to dump someone. Saturdays are ruled by Saturn. If you've ever seen the mythical image of Saturn wandering around with the hooded cloak and scythe, you'll understand. No one wants the Grim Reaper around when she's trying to attract love.

℮ ℮ ℮

Candle spells are all-purpose, everyday affairs that don't require full regalia. Casting a circle isn't necessary. But if attracting love is a very big deal for you, then I recommend doing it in a circle. Just remember to gather all your ingredients beforehand.

With the nail, inscribe the candle with the name of the person you want to attract. If you aren't focusing on someone specific, inscribe "The Perfect Mate" or something along those lines. Etch a few hearts, the Gebo rune X and the symbol for Venus while you're at it (see Important Stuff to Know, II). Any symbol that signifies love will help.

Anoint the candle wick to base with the oil of your choice and roll it in the orrisroot powder or the ground cinnamon. Set it in front of you and light it. Use the candle flame to light your incense.

Write down on your parchment or paper what it is you're trying to attract. You might write something like, "It is my deepest desire that _____ become filled with love for me. As I write these words I am already in his/her thoughts. The next time our paths cross he/she will be irresistibly drawn to me and wish to form a lasting relationship." What you write is totally up to you.

If you have a photograph of the object of your affection, hold it in your hand, gaze at it with intent, and repeat aloud what you've written on the parchment three times. If you have no photo, inscribe their name or "The Perfect Mate" seven times on the paper and repeat aloud what you've written. Kiss the picture and the paper, put them on top of each other so that your words are facing the photo or the names you've written, and slide all of this under the candle.

Now with every ounce of feeling you can muster, conjure up the spiritual presence of this person and "see" them sitting across from you. Hold that vision there as long as you want to and tell them what's in your heart.

When the thought transmission is complete, wait to see if you can hear them answer. You may hear many things. Don't discount any of them and whatever you do, don't listen to the little voice in your head that's telling you you're nuts to be doing this. The left-brain is the worst wet blanket when you're doing spell work. Hold the space of pure love until you're clear that the spell is complete.

Now snuff out the candle. Don't blow it out because this will blow all your wishes away. Leave everything where it is, and every day let the candle burn for an hour as you sit with it and focus your intentions. When there's nothing left, take the remains of the candle along with the picture and the paper, wrap them up in the pink cloth, and tie it with the string. Carry this pouch with you or keep it under your pillow. If it's possible, place the pouch somewhere where the object of your desire will step over it. You can bury it near the path that leads to their door, put it under their doormat, or even under their car mat, but you can't have anyone see you do this, and you can't have someone else do it for you.

Give this spell twenty-eight days to work. After twenty-eight days, bury the pouch in the North. Don't be discouraged if no one materializes. He or she will–probably when you least expect it.

A SPECIAL SPELL TO OPEN THE HEART AND ALLOW LOVE TO ENTER

Of course sometimes we don't have love in our lives because we've closed off our hearts. You know, we say we want to be in a relationship and we're mentally open to the idea of having a partner, but we've got this huge inner fear about really *receiving* love at the emotional level. Old patterns along with all the "blood on the tracks" make it hard for us to trust, and the fear of actually having to love someone and see ourselves in the process can be greater than the fear of being alone.

I don't care how much you like the thought of having a partner. Until you really feel in your heart what it will take for you to open up the vault and be receptive, love will not enter.

The "Let Me Be Open Enough To Let You In" Love Spell

What you'll need

A pink candle
Some rose incense
Rose oil
A nail
Matches
An apple
A paring knife
A piece of tumbled rose quartz
A glass of pure spring water
3 feet of pink rattail cord
Some string
A cup hook

Use the following spell on the day you wake up and realize that you're willing to go through whatever it takes to open your heart to love. The New Moon, the sixth day after the New Moon, or the Full Moon would be ideal for this spell. Any Sunday, Monday, or Friday under waxing lunar rays would be good too.

℮ ℮ ℮

I would do this one in a circle. It's definitely worth the time it will take to go through the steps to cast one. After all, most people don't realize their heart is blocked and the realization that it needs to open is a major epiphany. There's actually something sacred about it, so honor that sacredness with a circle.

Start this spell when the Moon is New. If you can work outside, do it. If you can work naked, do that also. Have all your ingredients ready and set your incense to burn.

Inscribe the candle with the words, "My Heart is Open." Anoint the candle, wick to base, with the rose oil, light it, and set it in front of you. Take the piece of rose quartz in your left hand and charge it with your intentions and your deepest wishes. The stone is alive and will hold those wishes for you. When you feel complete with this, drop the rose quartz into the glass of water. The energy from the stone will infuse the water with your vibrations.

Now cut the apple in half. Carve out the center of both halves of the apple and save the seeds. Place the apple halves next to the candle in front of you. Close your eyes for a minute and focus on your heart center. Visualize yourself being totally open to love. Surrender all fear and sense what it will mean for you to be receptive.

When you feel ready, open your eyes and say these words out loud:

> My heart is a clear vessel for light and love.
> With every breath I take, I feel the warmth of this
> feeling enter softly like a dove.
> From this moment on I am free of all fear,
> The Spirit of love fills me.
> Its sweet whisper is all I hear.

When you finish this invocation, sip all of the water out of the glass. Focus on the idea that every cell in your body is being "watered" with the consciousness held in your deepest wishes. Be careful not to swallow the rose quartz.

Now place the stone in the hollow you've carved in the center of one of the apple halves. Place the apple halves together so that the rose quartz is now inside the apple. Tie up the apple with the pink rattail cord like a pomander. Do this in a way that keeps everything together. Lay this charm next to the candle. Sit here for as long as you like.

Invoke all the angels that watch over you and ask them to help you remain open and receptive, knowing that your heart's desire is to know what it means to give and receive love. When you're finished and feel complete, snuff out the candle. Leave everything as it is on your altar. Release your circle.

Every night, light the candle and sit with it, holding the apple charm in your hands. When the candle is burned down completely, throw it into the nearest body of moving water. Bury the apple seeds in the ground. Take your charm, tie a piece of string to it, and hang it from the cup hook somewhere in your house or apartment that is special or sacred to you. Over time the apple will dry, but your intentions will always be held safely inside it.

You can charge this charm monthly at the New Moon if you want to. Sometimes it helps to remind yourself what it's there for.

SPELL TO REMOVE THE MENTAL BLOCKS THAT KEEP LOVE AWAY

Now it's all well and fine to open your heart to love, but if your mind is full of thoughts that say "You're too old" or "It's too late" or "Who would want you?" or even "Why bother?" nothing's going to happen. The mind is a huge magnet and whatever it's thinking will draw to you experiences that reflect and validate those ideas or beliefs that you hold about yourself. All of us are limited by what we allow ourselves to believe is true.

The "My Mind is a Magnet for Love" Spell

WHAT YOU'LL NEED

A magnet (a refrigerator magnet will do)
A white candle
A black candle
An orange candle
A mirror
Patchouli oil
Rose oil
A nail
Matches
Rose incense

A jar with a lid
A square of peach colored cloth and some pink rattail cord

———————————————

Use the following spell the minute you start to notice that your thinking patterns are running at cross-purposes with what your heart wants and what your Spirit came here to experience. Choose a Wednesday or a Friday to do this work. It would be ideal to start this one week before the New Moon and continue it through to the week after the New Moon. If this isn't possible, then just have faith that whenever you can do it is the perfect time.

ⓔ ⓔ ⓔ

Cast a circle and use your altar if you wish. Light your incense and let it burn. Place the mirror in front of you. With the nail, inscribe the white candle with the words, "My Mind is a Magnet filled with thoughts of Love," anoint it wick to base with the rose oil, and set it on the mirror to your left. Now inscribe the black candle with the words, "All negative thought patterns be gone!" anoint it base to wick with the patchouli oil, and set it on the mirror to your right. Light the white candle first and then light the black one. Now inscribe the orange candle with the words, "My heart's best interests fill my mind," anoint it wick to base with the rose oil, light it, and set it on the mirror between the white and black candles.

Put the magnet on top of your head and say these words out loud:

> *Every thought that defeats love*
> *Will fly away to the sky above.*
> *My mind is a magnet and can only see*
> *Thoughts that will draw love to me.*

Close your eyes and mentally release all the attachments that you have to the thought patterns that defeat your purposes as far as love is concerned. Feel the magnet on top of your head as an attracting mechanism that has the power to replace all those negative thought forms with positive ones. Feel your mind being filled with thoughts of love. Think of words like, "I am so lovable anyone would be lucky to have me" or "Love is a really important aspect of my life" or "A good relationship is essential to my growth and well being." What you choose to focus on is totally up to you.

When you're ready, open your eyes and gaze at the three candles in front of you. Visualize the flame of the black candle burning up all the old thought patterns and visualize the white candle giving life to thought patterns that will attract love to you. See the flame of the orange candle making it possible for you to watch over your thought processes and regulate any future negativity, if that becomes necessary. Stay in this space with the candles burning and repeat the words written above seven times.

When you feel complete, snuff out the candles. Leave them where they are along with the magnet. Burn the candles for a little while each night for the next two weeks. Place the magnet on your head every time you do this.

When the candles have burned down, put what remains of the black candle in the jar and place it behind you. Wrap up the magnet and what remains of the white and orange candles in the piece of peach-colored cloth. Tie up the cloth with the pink rattail cord and keep it under your pillow or mattress. Bury the jar with the remains of the black candle in the North.

THE AVOCADO CONNECTION

Avocados are little love machines. Who knew? We've been eating them for years and no one ever told us this. Avocado meat is reputed to induce lust if you eat it. If you mash one up and spread it on your face, it'll make you look young and beautiful enough to induce lust. Just remember to wash it off! Carrying an avocado pit in your purse is supposed to attract a lover, but the best thing to do with the pit is to sprout it and plant it. An avocado plant strategically placed in the right hand corner of your house or bedroom will draw love into your life. Here is another little thing you can do with an avocado pit that will bring love to you:

The "Avocado Love Charm"

<u>WHAT YOU'LL NEED</u>

An avocado pit
A band saw or hammer/chisel
Matches
A metal bowl and fireproof trivet
A kettle and water
A glass
A pink pouch or cloth

After you eat or use your avocado as a facial, cut the pit into four parts. This isn't easy. I do it with my boyfriend's band saw, but a hammer and chisel works well too. Burn one piece. Bury the second piece in the West. Throw the third piece off a high hill into a strong wind. Boil the fourth piece for ten minutes. Pour the water off into a glass and sip a little of it. Place the part of the pit that was boiled in the water into a pink pouch or tie it up inside a small piece of pink cloth. Carry this charm with you all the time or tie it to your bedpost. If you do this, you will never be without love that is strong and true.

ⓔ ⓔ ⓔ

SPELL TO TURN THAT FROG INTO A PRINCE OR PRINCESS

Sometimes not having a partner is not the problem, it's that our partners are half asleep or closed off in so many other ways. Whether we stand around making excuses for them or take a more proactive approach and bitch about them constantly, there's still a part of us that wishes they would magically transform and become everything we wish they were but aren't. I've noticed that this issue doesn't crop up as much in gay couples, but I've seen textbook cases of it among my lesbian friends, so I deliberately made the next spell gender neutral. Use it when you find yourself wishing that your partner was anyone but who he/she is, always keeping in mind that your partner is a mirror, and if you are unhappy with what you see in the mirror, you can *only* transform it by transforming yourself.

The "Only Love Will Fill Our Eyes" Spell

WHAT YOU'LL NEED

A mirror
A piece of parchment paper or
paper cut from a brown paper bag
Something to write with
3 or 4 tablespoons of red chili powder
A red pillar candle
Two poppets stuffed with ground coffee or black tea
A widemouthed jar with a lid
1 or 2 feet of red rattail cord
Musk oil
Musk incense
A nail

HOW TO MAKE A POPPET

Before you do this spell, you'll want to make your poppet. Poppets are used in all kinds of spells. Basically, a poppet is a little doll or effigy made out of cloth sewn together and stuffed with leaves or dried beans, in this case coffee or black tea. It doesn't have to be anything fancy. In fact, it shouldn't be. You can also make a poppet out of warm wax. Choose colors and characteristics that remind you of the person you are focusing on. If you don't sew, you can just pick up a little doll at the dollar store. Lemons will work too. If you use a lemon, stick whole cloves in it to create facial features. If you want to put big smiles on them or make them anatomically correct, go for it!

Start this spell at the New Moon and continue it for the two weeks leading up to the full moon.

℮ ℮ ℮

For this spell, you'll need two poppets (or lemons)–one to represent you, one to represent your honey. Cast a circle if you want to. Set the incense to burn. With the nail, inscribe the candle with the words "My love life is full of joy, passion, good communication, and fun." Carve your name and your partner's name on the candle too. Anoint it wick to base with musk oil, roll it in the hot chili pepper, and spark it up. Once it's lit set it on top of the mirror. Mirrors amplify energy and this spell is about amplification. The mirror will also serve to remind you that your partner is a mirror.

Now it's time to name your poppets. Write your name and your honey's on a piece of paper and cut out each one to pin to the back of one of the poppets, or you can just write your names right on the poppets if you'd prefer. Position the poppets so they face each other and tie them up with some of the red cord. Lay them on the mirror next to the candle.

Now write on the paper how you want your relationship to be. Go into as much detail as you want. Be specific. Read what you've written aloud three times, anoint the paper with three drops of musk, kiss it, and place it under the candle.

As you sit in front of the candle, meditate on the idea that you have chosen this person as your ideal mate. Know that whatever is manifesting in the relationship is something both of you have created as an opportunity to see yourselves and remember your oneness. When you feel ready, say these words out loud:

> In this moment I banish all needs to criticize.
> From now on when I am with my dearest one only
>   love will fill our eyes.
> In this moment I banish every feeling of fear.
> From now on our hearts will be open and our
>   words will be tender and clear.

In this moment there is nothing but love that
connects us heart to heart.
We are one and always will be. It's been that way
from the start.

Now put the poppets into the jar. Sprinkle the red chili pepper over them and close the lid. Now shake the jar a few times and place it on the mirror. Snuff the candle out and leave everything where it is.

Each night until the Moon is full, light the candle and let it burn for a while. Shake the jar with the poppets as you sit with the candle burning.

When the Moon is full, do one last candle burning, shake that jar up one more time, and read what is written above aloud three times. Take the paper from under the candle, fold it, and put it in the jar with the poppets and the chili pepper. Seal it all up tight and drip the wax from the candle over the lid. Snuff the candle and bury it in a spot that your sweetheart passes every day. Put the jar under their side of the bed. Leave it there till the Moon is new and then bury it where you buried the candle.

SIMPLE CHARMS TO
SPARK UP PASSION AND LUST

If your sex life could use a little spice–and whose couldn't from time to time?–you'll like these charms. If reigniting the spark in your sex life is a major concern, then I would recommend making these charms in a circle or on your altar. As you read through this section, imagine crone groups whipping up batches of these for the church bazaar instead of standard tea cozies and toaster covers!

The "Red-Hot Flames Of Passion" Charm

WHAT YOU'LL NEED

2 dried red-hot chili peppers, the longer the better
2 1/2 feet of red or shocking pink satin ribbon

This charm is for awakening lust. It looks a lot like a "God's Eye" and is just as easy to make.

I am assuming that everyone who reads this was a "hippie" in the '60s and knows what a God's Eye is. For those of you who don't, a God's Eye is something that you make by lashing two sticks of equal length together to form a cross. Bright, rainbow colored yarns are woven in and out of this matrix and a beautiful object is created that can be hung anywhere.

For the purposes of this charm, place the chili peppers on top of each other to form an equal-armed cross. Instead of using yarn, lash them together with the ribbon. Hang this charm from your bedpost and let it go to work. Make one for each side of the bed and it will work even better.

The "Cattails" Charm

WHAT YOU'LL NEED

10 Cattails
Red satin ribbon

In spell work, cattails are used to stimulate lust in a woman who has lost interest in sex completely. As I write this, I realize that the tips of these plants look like little penises so maybe that has something to do with it. Of course, if you're gay, penises aren't what get you going, but cattails could just as easily serve as reminders of the female genitalia. You'd have to live in a vacuum to make it through menopause and not know what the most common term of endearment for the female genitalia is.

I went through a year where sex was about as interesting to me as laundry and I made this charm to hang over my bed. All I can say is it seemed to help. Try out this charm if there's a glacier forming south of your navel.

Cattails grow everywhere, especially near swamps. If you can't find them growing nearby, you can buy some at the craft store or the florist.

If awakening lust is a big deal for you, go full tilt with casting a circle and work naked if you can. Otherwise, it's very simple. Just make a "bouquet" of ten cattails, tying them together with a red satin ribbon. Hang this over your bed or on the bedpost and leave it there to do its work. You can use the same cattails for up to a year, but it doesn't hurt to change them once a month.

HERBAL VIAGRA—GOLDENROD EXTRACT

I think it's interesting that the more sexually oriented the popular culture gets, the less sexy we become. You'd think with all the soft porn blaring at us from the media we'd be in a constant state of titillation. The opposite is true. In fact, lots of men seem to be getting to a place where their mind, their heart, and their penis no longer work as a team.

I have serious doubts about Viagra, but you can always count on Mother Nature to be there for you. This charm uses goldenrod as its main ingredient. Now close your eyes for a minute and picture the words golden rod. Hello! The connection here is obvious.

Goldenrod grows everywhere and is in season in August and September, sometimes even longer. Goldenrod starts to bloom when the Sun goes into the sign Leo around the last week of July and it stays in bloom longer than most plants. That's probably why it's so good for this particular ailment! If you can't wait for summer, then order it dried by the pound from your local health-food store or food co-op. For this extract, you'll want to use the whole plant.

Extracts are easy to make and definitely "witchy." If you whip up this batch of goldenrod extract, you'll have enough herbal Viagra to turn your kitchen into a "Lourdes" for all the men in your neighborhood who can't get it up.

The "Rise to the Occasion" Spell

WHAT YOU'LL NEED

A big, deli-sized dill pickle jar or
a five pound honey jar (glass is best)
Enough goldenrod to stuff and pack tightly
into the jar (whole plant)
Enough brandy, vodka, or grain alcohol to cover the goldenrod (If you're using a pickle jar you'll need a half-gallon and an extra fifth to do the job. If you use a honey jar, a fifth should do it. If you have alcohol issues, use cider vinegar. Organic is best.)

Stuff the jar as tight as you can with the goldenrod. If you're using fresh plants, use *everything*—roots, stems, flowers, and leaves. Fill up the jar with the liquor or the vinegar. Make sure there is no goldenrod showing above the surface of the liquid. Let this concoction sit for a month in a cool, dark place. Once a day, turn the jar upside down just to shake things up a bit.

At the end of the month, strain everything into another jar using a large funnel lined with a coffee filter or a piece of muslin. Pour the extract as needed into a brown stopper bottle and dose your man with fifteen to thirty drops under the tongue one or two times a day. You'll have enough to last you forever. Hopefully you won't need it that long, so share the wealth!

No chapter of love spells would be complete without a few for dealing with relationship endings. If you've ever had to end a relationship, you know how brutal it can be. Breaking up is hard for a lot of reasons. Your emotions can be pretty mixed. Anger and fear get all mixed up with hurt, sadness, and grief. If you've been with your partner for a long time, the whole idea that the relationship you've spent so much of your life nurturing is over can bring up all kinds of difficult thoughts. If you're the one getting dumped, then rejection will be a big piece of what you're dealing with, but it's just as painful when you're the one who wants out and your partner doesn't.

Endings are such a big part of life. Too bad we're not taught how to deal with them in school.

The following spells will help you through the rough spots the next time it's time to say goodbye.

The "Thanks For the Memories" Spell

WHAT YOU'LL NEED

A black votive candle
A white taper candle
Sage incense
Lavender oil
Ashes
3 tablespoons of dried dill
A photograph of the two of you together
Scissors
A widemouthed jar with a lid
A metal bowl and a fireproof trivet
Matches
A nail
Tissues

Parchment or paper cut from a brown paper bag
A black pen

This spell should be done in a circle, on a Saturday, when the Moon is waning. Whenever you want to banish anything, which would include ending a relationship, Saturdays work best. The dark of the Moon enhances spells of this nature, too, as the waning influence causes things to disappear.

℮ ℮ ℮

As soon as your circle is cast, light your incense and set it to burn. With the nail, inscribe the black votive candle with your name and the name of your partner. Anoint it base to wick with the lavender oil and set it in front of you.

Hold the photograph of the two of you together until you feel ready to cut yourself out of the picture and leave your partner by himself. Set the half of the picture that has your partner in it in the metal bowl. Now sprinkle the ashes over him and say these words out loud three times:

> I have loved you with all of my heart.
> As I say these words I know in my soul that the
>   time has come for us to part.
> I cherish what you have taught me and release
>   every need to hold on.
> Thank you for what you have brought me,
> But it's time for us to move on.

Now write a letter to your partner telling him everything you're thinking and feeling. Get it all out in the open, both the good and the bad.

When you're done, put three drops of lavender oil on the paper, fold it up, and kiss it once. Place it in the metal bowl with the ashes and their picture. Light a match and burn up what's in the bowl.

Focus your eyes on the flames and visualize the past and everything you associate with this person being gone forever.

When all that remains is ash, scoop it up and put it in the jar. Place the black votive candle inside the jar and seal it with the lid. When all the oxygen is burned up, this candle will extinguish itself. Watch this as it happens and wait for it to go out.

When this is complete, place the jar behind you. Now inscribe the white taper with the words, "Life goes on." Anoint it wick to base with the lavender oil. Light it and set it in front of you with the picture of yourself alone underneath it. Gaze at the candle and as you do, say these words out loud three times.

> *I am whole and complete and alive and real,*
> *Time will pass and my heart will heal.*
> *There's no need to dwell on the past and cry,*
> *Life goes on and so will I.*

Sit for a while in this space if you need to. When it's time, snuff out the candle and leave it where it is. Bury the jar that holds the past in the North. For a little while every day, burn the white candle and repeat the words written above three times. When the white candle is burned out completely, place it along with your picture in the metal bowl, sprinkle everything with the dried dill, and burn it all. Throw the ashes into the wind or into the nearest body of moving water.

SPELL TO GET RID OF THAT PERSON WHO JUST WON'T GO AWAY

There are other types of "endings," too, like when a suitor you have absolutely no interest in comes on to you and persists no matter what you say or do. It's awful to have to tell someone to back off. If you're polite about it, they rarely get the hint, and if you're not polite, it makes you both feel bad.

The easiest thing to do in this situation is feed him turnips every time he shows up at your house. I know, I know, it sounds weird, but it's an old wives' tale that's older than time itself, so there must be something to it. But since there's no way to guarantee that this will work or that he'll eat the turnips, it might be better to try the following spell. Before you do this type of work, however, make absolutely sure that you really do not want this person to bug you again, because believe me, he won't!

The "Don't Go Away Mad, Just Go Away" Spell

WHAT YOU'LL NEED

An orange candle
Patchouli incense
Patchouli oil
A whole turnip
A tablespoon each of lemon pepper, allspice, and fenugreek
A kettle with enough water in it to boil the turnip
A knife
A mixing bowl
Something to mash with
A nail
A widemouthed jar with a lid

You'll need to do this spell in your kitchen. If you want to do a makeshift circle around or near the stove, it can be done. This is practical magic, so don't worry too much about formalities. If the person you're giving the boot to is the persistent type, a circle will provide that extra kick.

This sort of work is always best done on a Saturday. Make sure the Moon is on the wane. It's OK if you can't find time to do this spell on a Saturday, but you should definitely do it when the Moon is waning.

℮ ℮ ℮

Light up your incense. With the nail, inscribe the candle with the words "Begone," "Out, out, damned spot," "Goodbye Charlie," or whatever floats your boat! Anoint it base to wick with the patchouli oil and rub a little of the allspice on it. Set the candle to burn on the table.

Now sit down with that turnip and carve into it the name of the person you're trying to get rid of. When this is done, chop it up and throw it into the pot to boil. While the turnip boils, mix the allspice, the lemon pepper, and the fenugreek seeds in the bowl. As you do this, see your partner/suitor/whoever getting the hint.

When the turnip is cooked, toss it into the bowl and mash it all up with the spices. *Don't* eat any of this or it will spoil everything. When it's all mashed to perfection, gaze at the candle for a few minutes and then say these words out loud three times:

> *I think it's time for you to leave.*
> *If you keep this up, you will only grieve.*
> *I no longer see your face at my door.*
> *As of this day, be gone and come no more.*

Put the mashed turnip and spice mixture in the jar. Let the candle burn until you feel complete. When the time is right, snuff it out and leave it where it is. Hop in your car and take a ride to the next town. Heading North is best. Find a place to bury the jar where no animal or human will dig it up. Walk away when you're done and don't look back. Every day burn that orange candle for a little while and repeat the above words three times. When it's all burned down, you should be free and clear. Bury the remains of the candle outside.

SPELL TO MAINTAIN A LONG DISTANCE RELATIONSHIP

A lot of us don't live with our partners. Sometimes that's a choice—maybe we found that playing house got old or we just needed space. There are also times when we have to separate temporarily because our work or our outside interests take us away from each other. Edna St. Vincent Millay wrote a little ditty that goes like this: "The fabric of my faithful love / No power shall dim or ravel / Whilst I stay here, but, oh my dear / If I should ever travel!" Doesn't that say it all?

The next spell is fun. If you have geographical fidelity issues, or if you've got an Internet love affair going, it'll come in handy.

The "Antidote for a Roving Eye" Spell

WHAT YOU'LL NEED

A map that shows where both of you are located
(You can draw your own if you want to)
White glue
Red glitter
Red-hot chili powder
Nutmeg powder
A Celestial Seasonings Red Zinger tea bag
2 pink candles
Musk oil
Orrisroot powder
Matches
A nail
Musk incense
A mortar and pestle or a bowl and wooden spoon

Pick a Friday when the Moon is waxing to do this spell. Friday's are ruled by Venus, and her influence opens the channel of love wide enough for a ley line to form between you and your lover. When that opening is clear, you don't need to be together physically to feel each other's presence. The forces of attraction need to be a strong as possible, so if you do this on the night of the New or Full Moon, it will be to your advantage.

Cast a circle if you want to pump up the volume. Gather all your ingredients together. Light the incense and with the nail, inscribe the candle that represents your mate with the words, "I only have eyes for you." Inscribe the candle that represents you with the words, "Love only me." Anoint each candle wick to base with the musk oil and roll each candle in the orrisroot powder. Place the candles on the map in front of you with each candle at the appropriate location. Light your candle first and then light your partner's candle. Now, in the mortar and pestle or bowl, mix up a tablespoon each of the nutmeg, the red glitter, and the red-hot chili powder.

Tear open the Red Zinger tea bag and toss the tea in with the rest of the spices. Add three drops of musk oil and a pinch of orrisroot to this potpourri. Stir it all up and with every ounce of intention you can muster, focus your mind on what you want. As you do this, say these words out loud three times:

> *There is no distance far enough to separate us.*
> *Our thoughts alone bring our passion to life.*
> *Whenever you think of me, you're filled with desire,*
> *To love any other would cause you nothing but strife.*

Now squeeze a line of glue on your map between your location and your lover's location. Sprinkle the mixture in the mortar and pestle over the little highway of glue. Sit there and remain focused on your intentions, let the candle flames burn, and wait for the glue to dry. When you're done, snuff out the candles.

Every day, sit in front of the map with the candles lit and repeat the above words out loud three times. When there is nothing left of the candles, bury them outside in the East. Keep the map under your pillow or under the mattress till your lover returns.

Here's a shorter version of the spell for those of you who don't have a lot of time or who just happen to be separated from the one you love because they're on a trip, in the service, or married! It's something you can do every day at sundown.

Stop for a minute and face whatever direction they're in. As you do this, say the following words out loud:

> *My love lies far beyond the Western (Northern,*
> *   Eastern, Southern) sky,*
> *Every day at sundown my heart does fly,*
> *Off with the crows whose eyes can clearly see,*
> *That every time I think of him he thinks of me.*

SPELL TO HELP YOU TELL WHICH SUITOR IS THE RIGHT ONE FOR YOU

The "Eenie, Meenie, Miney, Mo" Spell

WHAT YOU'LL NEED

A bag of onions
A paper bag
A nail

Having to choose between suitors—now that's the kind of problem I like! What follows isn't really a spell, but it's a good way to "divine" the answer to a question like this. Get a bag of onions. With the nail, inscribe the name of each candidate for your affections on one of the onions. Put all of the onions in a paper bag and stash them in a cool, dark place. Whichever one sprouts first is the man/woman of your dreams!

SPELL TO MAKE YOUR SWEETHEART WANT TO MARRY YOU

I have to admit this marriage spell is an afterthought. Personally, marriage makes absolutely no sense to me—I think it has as much to do with love as bad breath—unless there's a lot of money involved.

But who am I to judge? Some of you may have a more lyrical vision of marriage and if that's the case, this spell will help you prod your lover in that direction.

The "Bride of Frankenstein" (Heaven forbid) or "Let's Tie the Knot" Spell

WHAT YOU'LL NEED

2 pink candles
A nail
Matches
Rose oil
Rose incense
2 tablespoons orrisroot powder
3 one-foot long pieces of pink rattail cord
A pint-sized Mason jar
Enough spring water to fill it
A half-cup of sugar
A lock of your lover's hair. (If he/she is bald, a few pubic hairs will do. You'll have to do this while he/she sleeps because he/she can't know what you're up to. If you're the type of girl-friend who gives haircuts, you'll easily be able to save a lock or two of hair. Use your imagination and do whatever it takes. The old hairbrush is usually a good bet. If worse comes to worse, you can always check the shower drain.)
A lock of your own hair and ditto re: baldness!
A sprig of ivy and a sprig of holly

A New or Full Moon will work well, and if either of them falls on a Friday, you'll have it made. Venus's vibrations saturate the atmosphere every Friday. There's no better combination for a mat-rimonial spell.

℮ ℮ ℮

You will definitely need a circle for this one! Start your incense. With the nail, inscribe one candle with your name and one with your sweetheart's name and write "4 Ever 1" on both of them. Anoint each candle wick to base with the rose oil and roll them in the orrisroot powder. Light them and set them in front of you with your candle on the left and your partner's on the right. Place the holly next to your lover's candle and the ivy next to yours. As the candles burn, tie all the hair together with one of the pieces of cord.

Now add the sugar to the spring water in the Mason jar. Mix it well enough for the sugar to dissolve. Hold the lock of hair in your left hand and charge it with matrimonial imagery. When this is complete, pop it into the jar with the sugar and water. Now charge the holly and the ivy in the same way and put them in the jar too. When this is done, hold the second piece of rattail cord in your hand as you say these words out loud:

> We are lovers heart to heart,
> The time has come for us to wed.
> As I tie this knot, the magic will start,
> It's as your wife that I will share your bed.

With your clearest and firmest intention, tie one knot in the piece of cord and put it into the jar with the rest of the ingredients. Cap the jar, shake it once, and set it next to the candles.

Now tie the two candles together with the last piece of cord. Do this as best you can. They don't need to be joined at the hip any more than the two of you do!

Sit here with your thoughts filled with your deepest wish for as long as you need to. When you feel complete, snuff the candles.

Leave everything where it is and once a day until they're burned down, light the candles and focus on your wedding. When the candles are burned down to nothing, bury what's left of the candles and the jar in the North on the night of the New

LOVE (AND SEX) IN THE TIME OF THE CHANGE

or Full Moon. You should get your wish. If you don't, don't push your luck. You may be asking for trouble. After all, everything is in divine order and you can really make a mess of your life by forcing your will too strongly on any situation.

CHAPTER 5

Spells for Healing & Soothing, Ourselves & Others

Healing has always been a woman's art. Before males took over the medical establishment, it was women who practiced midwifery and cared for the sick. The ones who were good at it were called witches. During the Inquisition, any woman's knowledge of plants, herbs, and planetary rhythms made her suspect. Since that time, medical practice has become so organized and hierarchal, we've completely lost touch with the fact that all of us have the power to heal ourselves.

It's also a widespread belief that illness is something we "catch" or that attaches itself to us. This makes it seem as if we are separate from our ailments, that they are external forces that have nothing to do with us. It pretty much absolves us from having played any part in contracting the illness. It's easier to hand the healing process over to a doctor when you're programmed to believe that only an outside expert knows how to remedy the awful thing you've caught.

In the last twenty or thirty years, the viewpoint that all illness originates at the emotional level has gained momentum. We have learned that the physical, emotional, mental, and spiritual aspects of our being are all connected. Whenever any aspect of who we are in totality is out of synch, the imbalance will pop up at the physical level. What manifests physically is now viewed by many of us as a key that will help us to unlock the emotional/mental/spiritual causes that underlie it. Seen in this light, all illness is actually a gift and can be used as a tool to help heal ourselves.

Healing spells can help. They're not, of course, capable of healing anything by themselves. If the problem has taken a lifetime to finally reach the surface, once around with a healing spell won't make it go away any more than three "Hail Mary's" and an "Our Father" will wash away your sins. Any spell's power comes from the fact that you are taking the time to focus your heart and your mind on whatever the condition is. I believe that when the heart and the mind are focused with love and pure intention long enough, you can heal anything.

Because you're a woman, you're going to have a burning desire to heal everything in sight. Believe me, it's better to focus on healing yourself. For starters, directing a healing spell toward another person messes with their Karma. But if you *do* decide to do healing work for someone else, please meditate for a few minutes before you do the spell and *ask* their Higher Self for permission. If you get a "no," stop right there. If you get a "yes," go ahead. The best way to direct healing energy to another person is to simply pray for the Light to shine brightly enough within them to show them how to heal themselves.

SPELL TO HEAL THE PAIN
OF LOSING SOMEONE YOU LOVE

By now all of us have had to put someone's memory to rest, either because they died or because they walked out on us. If you've somehow reached cronehood without losing someone you love, you must live some sort of charmed existence. Emotionally it can take years to release a loss. Some of us never get over it. There comes a time when letting go of our pain is worth whatever it costs us to come to terms with it. This spell will help in any situation where you finally come to grips with the fact that in order to continue living, you have to say goodbye.

The "Goodbye Spell"

A poppet, a lemon, or a tiny doll
(see Chapter 4, p. 42 for instructions on making a poppet)
Patchouli oil
Your favorite incense
2 small white votive candles
An old mayonnaise jar or a widemouthed Mason jar
A handful of thyme
A dried bean
Ashes
A piece of black cloth
A box of tissues
A piece of parchment or paper cut from a brown paper bag
Something to write with
Matches

Do this spell when the Moon is waning. Remember, you're letting this person go and releasing all of your sadness and loss. The dark of the Moon will support your desire to let it all fade away.

℮ ℮ ℮

If it's important enough for you, cast a circle. Use your altar, too. If you start to cry at any point during this spell use your tissue and save those tears! You'll need them later. Before you get started, have your poppet (or doll or lemon) ready to go.

Set the incense to burn. Inscribe one candle with your name and one with the name of the person who's gone. Anoint them both base to wick with the patchouli oil and rub them with ashes. Light them and set them in front of you as you do the rest of the spell.

Write the name of your beloved on the poppet. Put ten drops of patchouli oil on the poppet and roll it in the ashes. Wrap it up in the piece of black cloth and hold it in your left hand for a few minutes or as long as you need to. As you do this, focus your thoughts on letting go of the need to hang on to them.

When this is complete for you, write whatever you feel called to write in the way of a "goodbye" on the paper. Read it out loud. Put ten drops of patchouli on the paper, kiss it once, and fold it up. Put the poppet in the jar along with the note.

Now charge the thyme and the dried bean in your left hand with love and understanding. Sprinkle the thyme over the charm in the jar and place the bean where the heart would be.

Set the candle that has your name on it inside the jar and screw on the lid. When the candle in the jar goes out, snuff out the second candle and bury the jar in the North or set it adrift on the ocean or any other body of moving water. Once a day, light the candle with your loved one's name on it and let it burn for a little while. When it's all burned down, bury it in the North along with the tissue and any of the tears you've shed.

SPELL TO HEAL
THE BODY AFTER MAJOR SURGERY

So many of us get to this point in our lives minus a few body parts. The physical self can change and be altered over time, but who we are essentially never changes. Even after death we go on forever. In this dimension, it's easy to believe that we are our bodies, but the body is just the vehicle that the soul works through. If you are about to go through or have gone through any sort of surgery, use this spell to remind yourself that you are whole and complete within yourself and that Spirit is what keeps shining through.

The "I Am Whole and Complete Within Myself" Spell

A pink candle
Rose oil
A nail
Sage to burn
A full-length mirror
A photograph of yourself
A glass of spring water mixed with a tablespoon of grenadine
syrup (if you can't find grenadine syrup,
substitute a glass of cold cider)
Scissors and tape
Matches
A metal bowl and a fireproof trivet

Doing this spell when the Moon is waning will make it easier for you to let go of the pain and any attachment to the part that's been lost.

℮ ℮ ℮

I would definitely cast a circle for this one. Go "whole-hog." It's a biggie. You might even want to work naked. Set the sage to burn. With the nail, inscribe the candle with the words "I am pure light" and anoint it wick to base with the rose oil. Sit in front of the mirror on the floor or in a chair and set the candle between you and your reflection. Cut from the photograph of yourself the parts of yourself that have been removed. Tape them to the mirror where they would be if they were still there. Gaze at your reflection until you are filled with the sense that this is *not* who you are.

Now turn your back to the mirror and bring the candle around too. Keep it in front of you. Gaze at the candle flame and breathe deeply ten times into your heart center. Rub three drops of rose oil into what's left of the photograph and set it alight with the flame. Burn the image of yourself in the metal bowl. Now say these words out loud:

> The clear light of Spirit, deep in my heart,
> Shines through all my losses and pain.
> The light of this candle
> And the Spirit within
> Is what glows and will always remain.

After a few minutes, when you feel ready, toast your Spirit with the spring water and the grenadine mixture or the cider. Feel it go all the way to the core of your being.

Now rub three drops of rose oil into each piece of the photograph that you taped to the mirror and burn them too. As you do this, know that they are always part of you on the etheric level but that the real essence of who you are is pure light.

Sit for as long as you want with the candle burning. Go into a meditation if you feel drawn to do so. When it's time, snuff out the candle and bring it to your altar. Burn it a little every day until it's gone. When it's burned to a nub, take a long walk and throw the remains off a hilltop into the wind or into any body of moving water.

SPELL FOR HEALING "CROSSED CONDITIONS"

We all get caught up in snares from time to time. Maybe there are bad vibes at home or at work, among friends, with relatives, with your partner, or even with yourself. Any situation, physical, mental, emotional, or psychological that is making you nuts is what I would call a "crossed condition"! Whenever things fall into a funk like that, use this spell to heal the situation.

The "Dissolve My Troubles Away" Spell

WHAT YOU'LL NEED

A white candle
A small black votive candle
A glass jar big enough to fit over the black candle
3 tablespoons of sea salt
Rose oil
Sage for burning
A piece of white cloth
1 or 2 feet of black rattail cord
Some rosemary
Matches
A nail
A metal bowl and a fireproof trivet

The waning Moon is best for a spell like this. When you wake up and realize it's time to kiss your troubles goodbye, you're basically banishing them. The fading light of the dark Moon will reinforce your desire to shake off these negative influences.

℮ ℮ ℮

Gather all your ingredients. Cast a circle if you want to. Set the sage to burn. With the nail, inscribe the white candle with words like, "Peace and Harmony," "Love and Light," or "Faith and Trust," whatever applies to your situation. Anoint the candle wick to base with the rose oil and light it up.

Inscribe everything you *don't* want in your life on the black candle. Try to summarize whatever this is in a word or two—after all, it's just a votive! Anoint the black candle base to wick with the rose oil. Set the black candle in front of the white candle and sprinkle the sea salt in a circle around it, keeping the white candle outside of the circle, to symbolically seal off the negative energy.

Light the black candle and understand that in doing so you are allowing yourself to shed light on the problem without getting sucked in by it. As you sit there gazing at both candles, tie a knot along the length of the piece of black cord for every issue that you have. Lay the cord around the black candle and say these words out loud:

> All of my troubles are held in this rope.
> They no longer bind me and my heart's filled with hope
> That the candlelight's glow will dissolve every fear.
> Nothing but Harmony can find its way here.

Now pick up the cord and untie every knot. As you do this, see all the crossed conditions coming unraveled. Focus on having everything be just as you wish for at least seventeen seconds.

Lay the cord around the black candle again, and sprinkle the rosemary over the cord. Put the jar over the black candle. When the flame goes out, cover the jar with the piece of white cloth.

Pick up the white candle and place it in front of you. Gaze at the flame for as long as you want to. When you feel complete, snuff out the white candle and set it on your altar. Wrap the jar, the salt, the rosemary, and the black candle in the white cloth, tie it with the black cord, and bury it outside where no animal or human will dig it up. Burn the white candle on your altar for an hour or so each day until it's gone. Then bury what's left of the candle it in the East, where the Sun rises.

SPELL TO SEND HEALING ENERGY TO SOMEONE ELSE SO THAT THEY CAN CONNECT WITH WHAT THEY NEED TO DO TO HEAL THEMSELVES

Anytime someone close to us is sick or suffering, it hurts. The instinct to "kiss everything and make it better" comes with the territory for most of us. By now we're all wise enough to know that we can't, and it's unethical to mess with people's karma anyway. This spell works in a way that helps the ailing person awaken to what they need to change in order for the pure light of Spirit to flow through and take care of the problem. It's just as applicable in situations where a friend or someone you love is being victimized by any form of abuse. Before you start, sit quietly and invoke your Higher Self. Ask if it's okay to proceed. You'll get an answer right away in the form of a feeling or a sensing that it's a good or a bad idea. If you get the go ahead, invoke the Higher Self of the person you wish to assist. Ask their higher aspect if it wants you to do this for them. You will know intuitively what the answer is. If the light is green, go for it. If it's red, forget the whole thing and know that time will show you why it's best to leave the situation alone.

The "May the Light Shine Brightly Within You" Spell

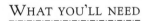

WHAT YOU'LL NEED

A white taper candle
6 white votive candles
A sheet of tinfoil
Lavender oil
A nail
A piece of parchment or paper cut from a brown paper bag
Something to write with
A poppet stuffed with rosemary or a lemon
(see Chapter 4, p. 42 for poppet-making instructions)
4 tablespoons of sea salt
Sage to burn
Matches

The New Moon is the ideal time for this type of work. When you do a spell at the New Moon, it marks the start of a two-week window where positive influences will increase. The energy you create with your love and good intentions at the New Moon will gain momentum and get stronger as the Moon reaches fullness.

℮ ℮ ℮

Cast your circle and use your altar if you feel it will help. Set the sage to burn and purify the space. Lay the tinfoil down flat in front of you to provide a surface on which to place your candles. The reflective energy of the foil will double your effort. With the nail, inscribe the white taper with the name of the person you wish to help. Anoint the candle wick to base with the lavender oil and set it in the center of the sheet of foil.

Now inscribe the six votive candles with these words: on the first candle write, "Love"; on the second, "Truth"; on the third, "Beauty"; on the fourth, "Trust"; on the fifth, "Harmony"; and on the sixth, "Peace." Anoint each votive wick to base with the oil.

Place the "Love," "Truth," and "Beauty" candles around the white taper in an upward-pointing triangle. Place the "Trust," "Harmony," and "Peace" candles around the white taper in a downward-pointing triangle.

Now write the person's name on the poppet or the lemon. Rub seven drops of lavender onto it. Now put the poppet next to the center candle. Light the six votives and sprinkle a circle of salt around everything to seal and protect the energy. On the piece of parchment or brown paper write these words:

> May the Spirit of the Archangel Michael
> Along with all the Higher Beings that watch over
>   my dear (the name of the person)
> Guide them safely through this test
> And open their eyes to the light so that the
>   wisdom in their heart will flower
> And show them what they need to do.

Place the paper underneath the center candle and the poppet. Light the white taper and meditate or pray in whatever way you choose until you feel complete. Snuff all the candles out one by one, leaving the center candle for last.

THE OLD GIRLS' BOOK OF SPELLS

Leave everything as it is and every day spend a little time burning the candles and praying for your friend or loved one. When every candle has burned down, wrap up what's left in the tinfoil, along with the poppet, and go bury it in the South where no animal or human will dig it up.

*(If it's your own sickness you wish to heal, you can use this spell. Just change the prayer by inserting the words "me" and "my" where appropriate.)

SPELL TO HEAL FEAR

At root, there are two emotions: love and fear. All other emotions derive from these two. We live in a polarized reality. Everything is understood relative to it's opposite. We are either feeling connected to life in a positive way or we are feeling separated from it. When we are in a state of connection, we are in love. When we are experiencing separation, we are in fear that we exist apart from everything. All the positive feelings such as joy, happiness, enthusiasm, and serenity are born out of love. All the negative feelings such hate, anger, selfishness, and depression are born from the fear that we are not loved by or connected to anything outside of our selves. Love connects us. Fear separates us.

When it comes to your health the fear that you might catch such-and-such an illness plays a big part in whether you do or not. This goes for everything from the common cold to cancer. The longer the fear is fed, the surer you are of attracting whatever you're afraid of. By the time you get to be our age, you may have been holding your fears for an awfully long time. This spell will assist you in releasing them.

The "There is Nothing That I Cannot Heal" Spell

WHAT YOU'LL NEED

A handful of dust from under the bed
A handful of ashes from the fireplace

A handful of dirt from a graveyard
Pieces of broken glass
10 common pins
Some spit
A mortar and pestle or a bowl and a wooden spoon
A blue bottle with a cork
A piece of parchment or paper cut from a brown paper bag
Something to write with
Patchouli oil
Patchouli incense
Rosemary oil
Sage incense
A black candle
A white candle
A nail
A piece of black string

Even though you're releasing your fears in this spell, you're also wanting to attract the most positive, healing vibrations. Do this spell on a Thursday or a Sunday when the Moon is waxing. That way the influence of Jupiter or the Sun will increase the light and love within your heart and give you the confidence to know that you really *do* have the power to heal anything.

℮ ℮ ℮

Gather all your ingredients together. Cast a circle if you want to and use your altar if you wish. Set the patchouli incense to burn. With the nail, inscribe the black candle with whatever you're afraid of and anoint it base to wick with the patchouli oil. Place it in front of you.

Mix the dust, ashes, graveyard dirt, pins, and pieces of broken glass in the mortar and pestle. As you do this, think about what you're afraid of and focus as intently as you can on connecting with the feelings that are fueling this fear. When you reach the point where you're clear about what this is, spit into the mortar and pestle and mix it in with the other ingredients.

Set the mortar and pestle next to the black candle and write down in your own words everything you can think of relating to where this fear comes from and why it's an issue for you. Rub the paper with ten drops of patchouli oil, form it into a makeshift funnel, and funnel all the other ingredients into the blue glass bottle. When everything's in the bottle, roll the paper into a scroll and tie it tight with the black string. Now cork the bottle.

Snuff out the patchouli incense and start burning the sage. Inscribe the white candle with the words, "I am the pure light within me." Anoint it with the rosemary oil wick to base, light it, and set it next to the black candle. Turn the black candle upside down in the mortar and pestle, snuff out the flame, and place it behind the blue bottle.

As you breathe in the sage, gaze at the white candle and say these words out loud:

> *I am the source of my life.*
> *Whatever I desire becomes real.*
> *The pure light of love has transmuted my fear,*
> *There is nothing that I cannot heal.*

Stay in this space for as long as it takes you to feel complete. You may want to meditate for a while. When you're ready to end this spell, seal the blue bottle completely by dripping the wax from the white candle over the cork. Snuff out the white candle and place it on your altar.

Bury the black candle and the bottle in the West, where the Sun goes down. Put a good-sized rock over the spot, walk away, and don't look back. Burn the white candle for a few minutes every night until it's gone. Cast the remains into the nearest body of moving water.

A BASIC HERBAL MEDICINE CHEST:
ECHINACEA, SAINT-JOHN'S-WORT,
AND VALERIAN EXTRACTS

When it comes to healing, everyone should have a few herbal extracts on hand. They're powerful allies for our bodies, they're easy and cheap to make, and they last forever. The three we'll be making here are the big guns of healing. First there's echinacea–the queen. Echinacea is wonderful. If you take it when you feel like you're coming down with something, it boosts your immune system and keeps you healthy. If you have a garden, you can grow it easily enough. It's a beautiful perennial. If you don't have a garden, you can order dried echinacea by the pound from any health food store or food co-op. Both the white and the pink varieties of this plant can be used for making extracts. Some people say just to use the roots of the fresh plant, but I use every part–roots, stems, leaves and flowers. I've done it the same way for years and my echinacea extract works like a charm! As far as dosages go, take thirty drops under the tongue, three times a day. You can put it in your tea, drinking water, or juice if the taste of the straight extract is too strong for you.

Then there's valerian. Valerian extract is great when you need to calm down. You can take fifteen drops sublingually or take it in tea. It is the remedy par excellence for the type of insomnia that comes with menopause, but any type of insomnia can be treated with valerian.

Some people will tell you to be careful about how you use valerian. In my experience, these are the same folks who will take piles of prescription drugs without batting an eye. The reason they tell you to be careful with this extract is because valerian is what Valium is derived from. I take valerian extract whenever I need to and all it does is help me sleep. I have never heard of it causing any negative side effects. The extract is a far cry from the drug, but if you're the cautious type, start out with fifteen drops and see how it affects you. I have more trust in Mother Nature than I do in the medical establishment, but if you feel you need to ask your doctor about using valerian, go right ahead.

Valerian grows in some parts of the country. You're more apt to find it in warmer climates. I've never grown it. I always use the dried root and I buy it by the pound because I also use it in my spell work. Unfortunately, it *stinks*. Really. It smells like stinky feet. But it's such a great herb that I overlook the way it smells.

The third healing extract of our trio is Saint-John's-wort. Saint-John's-wort has become very popular in the last few years as a remedy for depression. It has been touted as a substitute for Prozac and is a wonderful booster for the immune system. This herb grows everywhere. Around midsummer every year, it starts to flower in the gravel and in the dirt by the roadside and in the fields. Once you know what it looks like, you'll realize that you've been speeding past huge patches of it every time you're on the interstate. If you don't want to get out of your car and pick it yourself, you can order it by the pound at the health food store. When you do pick your own plants, use everything. The flowers, leaves, stems, and roots should be chopped up and stuffed tightly into a big pickle or honey jar.

I use the same basic recipe to make all these extracts. Here it is:

WHAT YOU'LL NEED

A big glass pickle jar or a five-pound honey jar
Enough of the herb packed tight to fill the jar
Enough brandy, vodka, or grain alcohol to cover the herb
(For a big pickle jar you'll need a big jug of liquor
plus another fifth to cover it all. If you have issues
with alcohol use organic cider vinegar.)
A funnel
A piece of muslin or a coffee filter
A small brown stopper bottle

If you're gathering your own herbs and you want to honor the lunar cycles, start this process right after the Full Moon. This insures that the extract will be loaded with the maximum amount of its natural properties.

Stuff the herb into the jar and pack it tightly. Pour the liquor or vinegar over everything. Make sure there's no herb showing over the surface of the liquid. Cap the jar really tight and let it steep for a month, turning it upside down once a day. At the end of a month, strain everything through a piece of muslin or a coffee filter placed inside a large funnel. Keep the strained extract in a jar and funnel it off as you need it into a small brown stopper bottle. The general dosage for this or any extract is fifteen to thirty drops under the tongue or in liquid three times a day.

Who knew that having this much power over your own health could be this easy?

CHAPTER 6

Protection Spells: The Witch's Stock in Trade

No matter how well armed we are against the vicissitudes of providence there are situations and people that can enter the picture and do a number on any one of us. Just the fact that we're females makes it more likely that we're familiar with being victimized, harassed, or abused. In any situation where your back's against the wall, there's often no recourse but to turn to a good protection spell, so it's wise to have more than one in your bag of tricks.

A protection spell is just what it sounds like: it casts a protective armor around you and shields you from negative energy of both the human and non-human form. Protection spells are the stock in trade for the practicing witch, and they're the basis for all witchcraft. I'm willing to bet that they come out ahead of love and money spells as far as the demand for them goes.

I chose to include the following protection spells because I've used them all myself at least once and I know they work. I have also passed them on to people who were in situations where they needed all the help they could get. At the etheric level, just the act of doing a protection spell liberates you from the negative energy that's being directed at you.

I hope that you never find yourself in a position where you have to use any of these spells, but if you do, here are the best ones I know.

THE "BOTTLE" SPELL

This is the all-time greatest, most useful protection spell. My friend Gretchen turned me on to it and I don't know where she got it, but Laurie Cabot also refers to it in her book *The Power of the Witch*. I'm pretty sure this spell has been in use for ages. What I love about it is that it allows you to neutralize the harm coming at you from outside influences without harming the forces that are causing the trouble. This is great because a white witch can never intentionally do harm without expecting to get that energy back in spades.

There are so many uses for the "Bottle" spell. It's great when you're having trouble with *anyone* who doesn't have enough class to treat you like a human being. I use it whenever someone is being a pain in the neck or when anyone is manipulating me in ways that are uncalled for. It's a subtle but effective tool that's bound to come in handy.

Usually when you're in the position to need this spell you don't have time to mess around looking for weird supplies, so I make sure to use ingredients that I don't have to go to great lengths to acquire. I include the original recipe just in case you want to go to the trouble of tracking down the orthodox ingredients, but next to the prescribed formula I include alternative ingredients that are easier to come by. The spell will work either way. Trust me.

WHAT YOU'LL NEED

4 tablespoons frankincense or myrrh
(4 tablespoons barley or burdock)
4 tablespoons powdered iron (an old iron nail)
4 tablespoons sea salt
4 tablespoons orrisroot powder
(4 tablespoons cornstarch or rice)
A white candle
A bottle with a cork or lid
A piece of parchment or paper cut
from a brown paper bag
A black pen

A piece of black string
Sage incense
A mortar and pestle or a bowl and a wooden spoon
Lavender oil

Do this spell on a Saturday when the moon is Waning to help limit and prohibit any outside influences and negativity. For a bottle spell to be effective, it's best to have the appropriate day and lunar phase. In an emergency, you will have no choice about when to do this spell and you'll just have to trust that it'll still work, regardless of the timing.

℮ ℮ ℮

Gather all your ingredients together. Cast your circle and set the sage to burn. Inscribe the white candle with the words "Darkness be gone" and anoint it base to wick with the lavender oil. Put the herbs, powders, salt, and the nail in the mortar and pestle. Mix them together with your thoughts focused on your highest wish. The idea is to infuse the ingredients with that intention. When you feel like this is complete, take the parchment paper and the pen and write these words:

> *I neutralize the power of so-and-so to ever do me*
> *any harm in this life or the next.*
> *So mote it be!*

Put four drops of lavender oil on the paper, form it into a makeshift funnel, and funnel the mixture from the mortar and pestle into the bottle. Kiss the paper to give it life, roll it up into a scroll small enough to fit into the bottle, and tie it with the piece of black string. Pop it into the bottle with the rest of the ingredients and cork the bottle or screw the lid on.

Now drip the wax from the candle over the top of the bottle as you turn it in a clockwise direction. This will serve to seal everything so that nothing can get in or out of the bottle.

Now take a walk or hop in your car and go into the woods. Bring a shovel along and dig a hole in the ground to bury the bottle. I like to bury my bottles under trees that have been struck by lightening for an extra-added kick. You know what they say, "Lightning never strikes twice in the same place." Your foe won't either!

After the bottle is buried well enough so that no animal or human will ever dig it up, point to the spot where you buried it with your right hand and say, "I wish for you what you wish for me." Then walk away and don't look back. I guarantee you will never be bothered again. The *only* thing that can mess this up is if something happens to the bottle after it's in the ground. I once buried a bottle way up in the woods and a few years later when they were logging the area the bottle was unearthed. Luckily, by that time, the person I bottled had made amends, and we were reconciled as friends again.

THE "RED CIRCLE" SPELL

This is the first protection spell I ever used. The great thing about it is that it requires no preparation or special ingredients and can be done on the spur of the moment. I found it in a weird old book. At the time my boyfriend's ex was being a *total* pain in the you-know-what and she just didn't know when to quit. I used this on her whenever she was acting up and it made my life so much easier. I *still* have the piece of paper with her name on it!

WHAT YOU'LL NEED

A 4-inch circle of parchment or
paper cut from a brown paper bag
A red pen

It helps to do any sort of banishing work on a Saturday, but people can hassle you *any* day of the week, so do this whenever you need to.

e e e

Inscribe a circle three inches in diameter on the piece of paper. Write the name of the person who's driving you nuts in the center of the circle. Lay the paper on the table and point at it with your right forefinger as you say these words out loud:

> *Evil return to source*
> *Impelled by incredible force.*
> *In the name of Tobeit (rhymes with "so be it")*
> *I am protected!*
> *So be it!*

Carry this piece of paper with you at all times and use it whenever you need to. The troubles you're being attacked with will get sent right back to the person who's giving you a hard time.

THE "HI-TEST" BOTTLE SPELL

When you get to the point where you feel all of your darker emotions coming to the surface and you just want to choke or castrate whoever's at the root of the problem, use this version of the "Bottle" spell. Some of you may find it too intense, but I have to say that there are certain situations where it's the first one that will come to mind.

WHAT YOU'LL NEED

A quart-sized, widemouthed bottle and lid
Pieces of broken glass and broken mirror, about a cup full
A cup full of sharp pins, nails, and pointed objects
A gallon of spring water
2 pieces of parchment or paper cut from a brown paper bag
A black pen

A black candle
Matches
Patchouli incense
A roll of toilet paper

_____

Always use a Saturday and a Dark Moon to do this spell unless it's an emergency!

@ @ @

An hour or so before you get started, drink as much spring water as you can.

When you are ready and have all your ingredients together, cast a circle, light the candle, and set the incense to burn. Hold the glass, the nails, and the pins over the candle with your left hand and after you charge them with your intentions, gently put them in the bottle.

On one of the pieces of paper, draw a circle and write the person's name inside it. Fold it up and put it in the bottle. On the second piece of paper, write down whatever it is that you need to vent and what you want to accomplish in your own words. Fold it up and add it to the bottle.

Now it's time to pretend you're going for a checkup and the doctor has asked you to bring a urine sample. That's right, you're going to pee in the bottle. If you read Louise Hay's book *Heal Your Body*, you know that anything to do with the urinary tract and what comes out of it has to do with anger and rage. Essentially what you're doing in this spell is drowning your enemy in your rage and releasing your anger in a way that won't make things worse. As you screw the lid on the bottle and seal all of your venom inside it, say these words out loud:

> *I send all your evil back to thee,*
> *May it never return to trouble me.*
> *There is nothing that you can do,*

To keep this wish from coming true.
So mote it be!

Now drip the black candle wax over the bottle so that nothing can enter or leave it. Take a walk in the woods or a drive in the country with a little shovel and bury the bottle deep in the ground. Stand over the spot where you bury it, point to the ground with your right forefinger, and say:

I wish for you what you wish for me.

As you walk away, without looking back say:

In no way will this spell reverse or cast upon me
any curse.

This last line, which I've borrowed from one of my favorite witches, Sybil Leek, insures that no harm will come from any of the energy you've unleashed. I have always followed her advice and added it at the end of any spell that has this kind of an edge to it.

COMFREY—FOR SAFETY AND PROTECTION WHEN YOU TRAVEL

Often when we get older, life opens up and we get to go places and do things we've never done before. I didn't leave the house in fifty-three years. Now all of a sudden I'm traveling all the time. If you travel a lot, have anxiety about taking a road trip by yourself, or are convinced that it's your flight that will dive bomb into the ocean on the way to Timbuktu, here are a couple of things that you can do.

If you are a gardener, you probably know what comfrey is. It's an amazing herb whose main property is its strength. Comfrey grows anywhere and will take over wherever it's planted. It has rejuvenation and longevity properties that may have something to do with the fact that from a magical perspective its most common use is as a "life preserver." When you travel, put some comfrey in your suitcase and carry-on luggage, and if you're driving, pop some in the trunk of your car. If you like, you can go "Martha Stewart" and make little sachets full of it just to avoid getting herbs in your undies. If you don't have any growing in your garden, you can find the dried herb at any good health-food store.

CHARM TO WARD OFF BAD DREAMS OR NIGHTMARES

When we go through menopause, night sweats, insomnia, and crazy dream patterns are part of life. As I see it, what's happening here is a reawakening of long-dormant psychic powers. You're not crazy, you're just busy tapping into aspects of yourself that were lost to you back in your teens. Or maybe you're lucky and your own sleep is fine, but you have grandchildren who wake up in the night in a state of terror. If any of these things is a problem, light a blue candle and as it burns fill a white or blue bag with morning glory seeds. Sprinkle ten drops of lavender oil into the bag, charge it in your left hand with thoughts of peaceful rest, and place it under your (or your sleep-disturbed loved one's) pillow. If you do this for one of your grandchildren, explain to them what it's for, and if you have any fear that they might open the charm and eat the seeds, tie it under the bed where they rest their head instead.

SPELL TO BREAK A BAD LUCK STREAK

Because of my astrological background, I know that there are times when our stars are just crossed. In fact, some planetary influences can hold things up for years, and many of the most hair-raising astrological transits don't even kick in till you're between forty and sixty. The ones that create the most upheaval last between a year and three years. Longer term progressed aspects can impact an individual indefinitely. I like the expression, "Consider the uses of adversity". Thank God by the time you're a crone, extended periods of difficulty don't surprise you as much as they did when you were younger and more naïve. Age teaches you how to hunker down and gather strength for the long haul. Wisdom helps you cope with it.

It's important to remember that long before we came here, we chose our karma and made a contract to experience whatever it is that comes our way. From a higher perspective, what we term "bad stuff" has a purpose, but when you're in the middle of a long run of bad luck that perspective can easily get lost.

This spell is a great way to remind yourself that the down periods of your life are more valuable than the times when everything's going great. It includes a psalm that will give you the strength to persevere in spite of conditions that appear to be conspiring to rob you of your faith. I'm including it in this chapter of protection spells because sometimes we need to protect ourselves from our own negativity.

The "B.B. King, Born Under a Bad Sign" Spell

WHAT YOU'LL NEED

A white candle
Matches
Lavender oil
A Bible
A piece of parchment or paper cut from a brown paper bag
A red pen
Frankincense or sage incense

Pick a Saturday when the Moon is waxing to do this work. In a spell like this, there's a mixed bag of energy going on. On the one hand, you're trying to release a lot of heavy stuff and the pressure it's creating and on the other, you're trying to pump yourself up enough to deal with it. Saturday's influence will help to lessen the weight of your problems, and the force of the waxing Moon will help you gather inner strength.

Cast a circle and light your incense. Anoint the candle base to wick with the lavender oil and light it. Draw a four-inch square on your paper. Write your name and draw your zodiac symbol inside this square. Put three drops of lavender oil in the center of the square. Set this seal next to the candle and repeat the Ninety-first Psalm three times. Here is the King James version:

> He that dwelleth in the secret place of the most High shall abide under the shadow of the Almigty. I will say of the Lord, He is my refuge and my fortress: my God; in him will I trust. Surely he shall deliver thee from the snare of the fowler, and from the noisome pestilence. He shall cover thee with his feathers, and under his wings shalt thou trust: his truth shall be thy shield and buckler. Thou shalt not be afraid for the terror by night; nor for the arrow that flieth by day; nor for the pestilence that walketh in darkness; nor for the destruction that wasteth at noonday. A thousand shall fall at thy side, and ten thousand at thy right hand; but it shall not come nigh thee. Only with thine eyes shalt thou behold and see the reward of the wicked. Because thou hast made the Lord, which is my refuge, even the most High, thy habitation; There shall no evil befall thee, neither shall any plague come nigh thy dwelling. For he shall give his angels charge over thee, to keep thee in all thy ways. They shall bear thee up in their hands, lest thou dash thy foot against a stone. Thou shalt tread upon the lion and adder: the young lion and the dragon shalt thou trample under feet. Because he hath set his love upon me, therefore will I deliver him: I will set him on high, because he hath known my name. He shall call upon me, and I will answer him: I will be with him in trouble; I will deliver him, and honour him. With long life will I satisfy him, and shew him my salvation.

Go into a meditative state for as long as you want to. If this feels foreign to you, just gaze into the candle flame. When you're ready, snuff out the candle and leave everything where it is.

Once a day, light the candle for a period of time and read the Ninety-first Psalm aloud three times. When there is nothing left of the candle, bury the remains and the seal far away from your house.

WOLF'S HAIR

Wolf's hair is the greatest thing in the world to protect yourself with. I have a friend who raises wolves and whenever I need wolf's hair, I go to his house and gather all the hair that his "babies" have shed. He used to save bags of it for me until he got the idea to spin it into yarn and make a wolf's hair sweater for himself. I keep a big jar of wolf's hair in the cupboard and give it away to people who are in really dire straits. If you feel like tracking down people who are into wolves, it's not that hard to do. They're around and usually happy to give you as much fur as you want.

Wolf's hair carried in a red cloth pouch will protect you from anything. You can make little bags of it to give away. When you or someone you love has to undertake anything dangerous, this is the best thing to carry. If there aren't any wolves in your neck of the woods, use the hair of a black dog. It will work just as well.

SPELL TO HELP YOU DEAL WITH YOUR OWN OR SOMEONE ELSE'S POWER ISSUES

In any group of powerful females, there's bound to be some competition and envy. In crone circles, the main point of envy is power, and power manifests at a lot of different levels. People can feel envy toward our success, our money, our relationships, our beauty, our position, or our abilities, you name it. It's much better when this stuff is brought out in the open, but it's more likely that it won't be. When there are subconscious power trips going on with those closest to us (as in sisters, mothers, in-laws, neighbors, friends), it's even more complicated! If you can recognize these things and deal with them openly and honestly you're fortunate. When you can't be up front about envy, jealousy, and other sorts of power issues, there are other ways to take care of it.

What follows are two spells that you can use to dissipate any kind of power issue between you and anybody else.

Spell to Dissipate the Force of Someone Else's Envy or, The "Get Off My Case" Spell

WHAT YOU'LL NEED

A black candle
A white candle
Matches
Patchouli incense
Patchouli oil
Rose oil
A piece of parchment or
paper cut from a brown paper bag
A pen
A nail
2 feet of string
2 hard-boiled eggs

Pick a Saturday under a waning Moon to do this spell. Remember, Saturdays are ruled by Saturn, and Saturn makes things disappear. In this situation, your desire is to lessen the effects of someone's envy or jealousy. The waning Moon is always great when you need to make something go away. It will provide an extra kick and help you to get whoever's on your case to get off it a lot quicker.

℮ ℮ ℮

You can cast a circle for this or not; it's up to you. Gather all your ingredients together, and set your incense to burn.

With the nail, inscribe the black candle with the name of your friend, enemy, or family member along with one word that signifies what it is you have that they want. Inscribe the white candle with your name and the words "Free and Clear." Anoint the black candle base to wick with the patchouli oil. Anoint the white candle wick to base with the rose oil. Set the white candle in front of you to the left of the black candle and light them both.

Write your name on one of the hard-boiled eggs and set it in front of the white candle. Write the name of the other person on the second egg and place it in front of the black candle. Peel the second egg, put the eggshell behind you, and carefully remove the yolk, preserving the white and making sure to keep the yolk whole. Place the yolk between the two candles.

Now write on your parchment or paper in your own words whatever the issue is. Anoint the paper with three drops of rose oil and three drops of patchouli oil. Read what you've written aloud three times, kiss it once, and place the paper under the egg yolk. Sit for a few minutes gazing at the candles and when you're ready, say these words out loud:

> What I have and what you want from me
> Is already yours but you cannot see
> That all of us have within our Being
> The things we lack and are not seeing.
> Reclaim what's yours and hold it near,
> My gift is your gift, now my dear.

Take the egg yolk and replace it inside the white. Wrap the peeled egg in the piece of parchment and tie it up with string. Bury this charm and the discarded shell near the person's house. If they live at a distance, bury everything in the direction where they live. Anoint the egg that is intact with rose oil and bury it in the North. Snuff the candles out and burn them once daily. When you do this, repeat the spell written above three times. When the candles have burned down to nothing, bury them in the North where you buried your egg.

Spell To Dissipate Your Own Envy, or The "Hasta La Vista, Green-Eyed Monster" Spell

WHAT YOU'LL NEED

A black votive candle
A white candle
Matches
A nail
A jar
A piece of parchment or
paper cut from a brown paper bag
Musk oil
Rose oil
A pen
Spit

You will need to do this spell on a Saturday when the Moon is waning. Waning lunar energy and the Saturnine vibration that rules Saturdays are perfect for releasing all forms of negativity.

℮ ℮ ℮

Gather all your ingredients together and cast a circle if you wish. Light your incense. With the nail, inscribe the white candle with the words, "I am whole and complete" and anoint it wick to base with the rose oil. Inscribe the black candle with the word or words that best signify what you feel you want from the other person and anoint it base to wick with the musk oil. Light both candles and set them in front of you with the white candle to the left of the black one.

Let them burn, and as they do write in your own words whatever the issue is on the piece of paper. Set the paper between the two candles and anoint it with nine drops of each oil. When you feel ready, say these words out loud three times:

What I desire of yours is mine I see
My envy keeps it away.
Now that I know how I need to be
My jealous heart has nothing to say.

Fold the paper and put it in the jar along with the black votive candle. Spit ten times into the jar, screw on the lid, and seal it with wax from the white candle. Snuff out the white candle and leave it where it is.

Take a walk with the jar. Go someplace where there are a lot of rocks and throw the jar at them as hard as you can. Turn your back on your envy and as you do say,

In no way will this spell reverse or cast upon me
any curse.

Every day until it's gone, burn the white candle for at least a few minutes and repeat the entire invocation three times out loud. When the candle has burned down completely, bury it in the East.

KEEPING BAD NEIGHBORS AWAY

Bad neighbors come in all shapes and sizes. There are the kind I call "coffee beggars" or "time-sucking voids" who won't leave you alone. They're always calling or "popping in" to waste your time. Then of course there are the ones who are just beyond obnoxious, the ones who are into all kinds of weirdness or who are just plain dangerous. The simplest, most effective way to protect yourself against bad neighbors is to cast a circle of sea salt around your property once a month just after the Full Moon.

If you have a *really* bad situation going on, it's well worth it to order a pound of dried valerian root at the health-food store and mix it with enough sea salt to do the job. The amount of sea salt you use will depend on the size of your property. If you live on a hundred acres of land, then I would suggest just surrounding the house itself with the valerian-sea-salt mixture.

Nothing and *no one* will bother you again. If you live in a condo or apartment building, all you have to do is mix up equal parts of sea salt with ashes and sprinkle it around your doorway, around their doorway, and/or under both doormats just as the moon begins to wane.

CHAPTER 7

Home and House Spells and Blessings

You may have noticed that I didn't include too much about house protection in the previous chapter. That's because I thought the subject of keeping our homes clear of negative energy deserved a chapter all its own, especially now that we're older and the vibes around the house have undoubtedly changed as our kids have moved out and taken all their noise and comings and goings with them.

When we hit menopause, our homes often become ours for the first time, and instead of vibrating with all kinds of activity they turn into more of a sanctuary where we go to regroup or fall apart if we have to.

Most of us want a place where we can focus our creativity and locate the deeper meaning in what half a life has taught us. So keeping the energy clear at home is essential. Our inner emotional state depends on it and *everything* else that goes on around us is a direct result of whether or not that internal balance is being maintained. So this chapter is devoted to spells for keeping our homes clear of negative energy.

Before you do *any* of the spells in this chapter, I highly recommend that you hire someone to come to your house and dowse for geopathic stress running through your property. This technique will clear your space of any and all negative frequencies created by the increased use of electrical power on the planet. It won't matter how many circles you cast or how much sage you burn–if there are geopathic stress lines criss-crossing through your house, no spell you do will have any effect in the long run. If you want to find out more about geopathic stress, go to Slim Spurling's website at www.slimspurling.com. Slim is the Merlin of geobiology and a fore-runner in this field.

Once you clear the geopathic stress, a little feng-shui would help too. Feng-Shui is so popular right now, you may already be using it. If not, find out as much as you can on the subject and experiment on your own or hire someone to come in and feng-shui your house.

The following spells and rituals will help you bless, clear, or even exorcise your space if need be.

A HOUSE BLESSING

If you're moving into a new house, it's a good idea to formally bless the space you're in. You can do this on your own or turn it into a party. House blessings are in vogue right now. It's a really nice custom, particularly because any move is a big psychological milestone, and the moving we do at our age is usually attended by major revelations about who we are and what we would like to become. Many of us are closing the door of the past, for one reason or another. The idea here is to set your intentions for your new life and honor the fact that this new place will be the "womb" that those intentions take root in.

The "Bless This House" Spell

WHAT YOU'LL NEED

A small table to use as an altar covered
with your favorite colored cloth
2 cups of sea salt
As many white candles as there are
occupants in the new house

Rose oil
Rose incense
3 tablespoons of cinnamon
A bottle of red wine and as many glasses
as there are people present
A big pot filled with 3 onions, 3 lemons, 3 garlic heads,
3 cinnamon sticks, a penny, and enough water to cover
everything (peel and chop the first three ingredients first)
A piece of parchment or paper cut from a brown paper bag
A pen
A nail

A New Moon is great for a house blessing because it's rays enhance any new beginning.

℮ ℮ ℮

Before you do this spell, boil the pot full of water and all of the pot ingredients on the stove. Once it's going, turn the flame way down and let it simmer.

When you're ready to start your houseblessing, gather all the other ingredients on the table. Take the two cups of sea salt and sprinkle a little into every corner of the house. Start at the North and move through the house in a clockwise motion going into every room. Light your incense and with the nail, inscribe each candle with the name of each person who will be sharing the house with you.

Starting with your own, anoint the candles wick to base with the rose oil and roll them in the cinnamon powder. Set them up in a circle on the table and light them from the same match if you can. Give yourself a minute, and as you soak up the candlelight and the aromas filling the atmosphere, say these words out loud:

My search for harmony has brought me here,
After years of wandering I no longer fear,
What it might be like to live free and clear.
These walls will bear witness to my new start,
In my new home, in my new heart.
Nothing can destroy or take away,
The blessings being born in this house today.

Now crack open the wine and raise your glass to your new life. If you're alone, write down on the parchment whatever your Spirit feels called to write. I'll leave that up to you. If you have company, pass the paper around and have everyone offer a word or a blessing. Anoint the paper with the rose oil, kiss it once, tear it into small pieces and put it into the pot on the stove. Stir everything well and when it feels "cooked" go outside with this "stew" and pour it around the front doorstep or around the perimeter of the house.

Go back inside and have a party and dance or just hang out by yourself, soaking up all the good vibes. Let the candles on the table burn down to nothing. When the flames are gone, take the candles and bury them outside your door.

Now, grab your broom, sweep up all the salt and sprinkle it around the outside of the house.

Whatever intentions you gave birth to on this day have entered every nook and cranny of your new space. Get ready for your new life and be happy knowing that everything you wish for will probably come true.

PLANTS AND AMULETS TO PROTECT YOUR HOME AND PROPERTY

Our ancestors knew a lot about protection, and most of the superstitions that have been passed down have their basis in older magical traditions that have remained alive and in the background in spite of the Inquisition. I live in New England and everywhere you travel there are lilacs growing. They were planted in the old days to protect the house from harm. The same goes for elder trees and hydrangeas. Elder trees were deliberately planted to protect the home from lightening strikes. That's why in some old magical traditions it's illegal to burn elder wood. If you are buying property or making changes to your current property, I highly recommend planting these trees and shrubs at the corners of your house and at the four directions.

Hawthorne trees and mountain ash, or rowan, trees are really good for protection, too, as are geraniums. Geraniums keep any sort of evil away and are used to ward off snakes. This includes two-legged reptiles. Geraniums thrive despite neglect so even if you don't have a green thumb they'll keep growing. You can keep them on your porch and fill your windows with them.

If you live in the Southwest, cactus plants can be used for protection around the home and on the doorstep. Anything with sharp spines acts like a little sword and the plant becomes a sentry whose sole purpose is to guard your home.

Wherever I live, I use horseshoes around the house. We're all familiar with the image of a horseshoe tacked over the door. This sends all forms of evil and negativity out the way it came. If you "plant" four horseshoes at the North, East, South, and West corners of your property it's even better. Just be sure the open end of the horseshoe faces out. Sometimes I use old rail spikes in the same way. If you live in a condo or rent an apartment, you can do this too either inside your space or outside on the grounds.

It also helps to sprinkle sea salt in a circle around your property from time to time. I do it whenever my neighbors–or anyone else!–are driving me nuts. Which gets me to another point: If you're renting a house that's up for sale and you don't want it to sell until *you're* ready to move, mix a bag of sea salt with a pound of fresh or dried valerian root. Sprinkle it around the property. No one will buy the house until you're ready. Sea salt alone will work if it's sprinkled with clear intentions. Just be sure to walk the property in a clockwise direction.

SPELL TO RESTORE PEACEFUL
VIBES BETWEEN FAMILY MEMBERS

Sometimes it's not your house but the people inside it who are creating a lot of negative energy. If you wanted to, you could "Bottle" your relatives (see Chapter 6, p. 76), but it's not really kosher to do that unless they're dangerous. If your partner, your kids, your mother, your mother-in-law, your wayward brother-in-law, or your schizophrenic dog are making the atmosphere less than harmonious at home, use the following spell. It'll help you stay centered and focused even when they aren't.

The "Goodbye Bad Vibes" Spell

WHAT YOU'LL NEED

A blue pillar candle to represent peace
A white candle to represent you
Floating tea candles for each person who's driving you nuts
A big pot of chamomile tea
A bowl big enough to float the candles in
4 tablespoons of sea salt
Rose oil
Lavender oil
Rose incense
A piece of blue rattail cord
A quart-sized Mason jar
A nail

Do this spell just as the Moon starts to wane. The bad vibes will diminish just as the lunar rays do. By the time the New Moon rolls around everything should be totally blissful.

☙ ☙ ☙

Gather all of your ingredients, cast your circle, and light the incense. With the nail, inscribe the blue pillar candle with the words "Peace and Harmony" and anoint it wick to base with lavender oil. Set it in front of you. Carve your name into the white candle and anoint it wick to base with the rose oil. Place this candle next to the blue one. Light the blue candle first and use its flame to light your candle.

Place the bowl in front of you and fill it with the chamomile tea. Sprinkle a circle of sea salt approximately 20 1/2 inches in diameter around this arrangement, starting at the North and moving clockwise. Take all the tea candles, inscribe each one with a name, and place a drop of lavender oil on the bottom of each one. Line them up in a ring *outside* of the circle of salt and light them one at a time, always moving clockwise. As you sit with everything burning, say the following words out loud seven times:

> My home is a haven of peace and love,
> A choir of angels has come from above
> To watch over and influence everyone here,
> Joy and laughter now replace trouble and fear.
> All the bad apples have changed their tune,
> We'll be getting along fine by the next New Moon.

When you're done reciting this rhyme, float the tea candles one at a time in the bowl of chamomile tea. Let everything glow and burn until the tea candles go out. As soon as they do, pour what remains of them along with all of the tea into the Mason jar. Tie the rattail cord tightly around the jar and leave just enough cord free to hang it up from a closet pole in the back of one of your less frequently used closets. Let it stay there forever if need be.

Every night till the Moon turns New, re-light the white candle and the blue candle, let them burn for a while, and repeat the words written above silently or out loud. When both candles are nothing but a pile of wax, bury them in the West. Things will improve gradually over the next two weeks. You might even notice a difference right away. Even if the people who drive you crazy continue to be obnoxious, you won't be bothered by their behavior.

CLEANSING AND PURIFICATION TECHNIQUES TO USE ANYTIME THE VIBES AT HOME FEEL LESS THAN HEAVENLY

It's a good idea to "clear" your space at every Full Moon. All kinds of things can disturb the general vibes in your home. Fights or visits from people who show up and leave a truckload of bad vibes, among others. If you or someone you live with has been ill for a long time the atmosphere can get messed up too. Whenever you notice that your space feels murky, use these tricks to clear things up. You'll probably want to use this spell on a regular basis if you are someone who's really sensitive to energy.

The "Clearing the Vibes" Spell

WHAT YOU'LL NEED

2 lemons for each room of your house
A knife

Cut the lemons in half and place a half in each corner of every room. Watch and see what happens. Sooner or later they will turn black. Believe it or not, this sometimes happens within an hour or two, especially if there's been a lot of fighting or when someone's been sick.

Just keep an eye on what the lemons are doing and remove them as soon as they turn black. You may have to do this clearing twice to really do the trick, but you'll notice that things feel 100 percent better afterward. Bury the lemons along with all the bad vibrations outside in the North corner of your property.

@ @ @

Vibe Clearing, Part Two

WHAT YOU'LL NEED

3 pounds of sea salt
A bucket
Cedar chips

A simpler way to clear your space is to mix three pounds of sea salt in a bucket with enough cedar chips to fill the bucket. Sprinkle this mixture on the floors in every room except where you have wall-to-wall carpet. Let the energy of the salt and cedar soak in for an hour or even longer if you have time for it. When you're ready, sweep up everything and toss or bury it.

CLEANSING RITUAL TO RELEASE WAYWARD GHOSTS

Releasing wayward ghosts isn't as far-fetched as it seems. There are legions of spirits stuck in the nether regions of the astral plane. The world is more heavily populated with invisible entities who don't know enough to move on than it is with flesh and blood humans! Whenever someone passes on, it's easy for them to want to stay close to the people and places they love. Those spirits who get pulled out of 3D suddenly often don't even realize that they're dead and they continue going about their business just as if they were still alive.

If you're sharing your space with an invisible roommate, it will be better for both of you if you help him or her move on. The following procedure is very simple and useful for dealing with benign entities. If your spooks are less than cheerful, this technique won't do the trick. You'll need to hire a professional to come in and do the job for you.

The "Ghost Buster" Ritual

WHAT YOU'LL NEED

2 pounds of sea salt
A white candle
Rose oil
A nail
A smudge wand of sage and cedar
A heart full of love

A ritual like this can be done just as the Moon begins to wax or just as it starts to wane. It depends on how you look at it. On the one hand, the waning Moon is appropriate because you're making this entity go away. From the spook's perspective however, it's a new beginning, so if you see it that way, the New Moon would work just as well.

℮ ℮ ℮

When you do this ritual you need to be coming from love instead of fear or anger, so see the Spirit you're helping to escort out of your house as if they are a lost child looking for their way home. Before you start, take the bag of sea salt and starting at the North, walk around your house in a clockwise direction sprinkling the salt in a circle of protection. When you go back inside, open all the windows a crack. With the nail, inscribe the name "Archangel Michael" into the white candle, anoint it base to wick with rose oil, and set it on a table in the middle of the house. Whenever an entity sees the Archangel Michael, whose emanations are of pure unconditional love, he knows he's safe and it fills him with trust and faith.

Light the smudge stick and carrying the candle, move clockwise from room to room letting the smoke purify each space. As you do this, say these words out loud:

Spirits be gone!
Return to thy place,
Leave peace to reign in time and space.
The Archangel Michael surrounds you with love,
He's waiting for you to fly far above.
Follow his light and follow his hand
He'll take you to the promised land.

After you've gone through every room, take the candle outside, hold it up to heaven, and repeat the words written above until you're clear that this Being has moved on. Snuff out the candle and bury it in the North. Once it's in the ground, place a rock over it.

SPELL TO HELP YOU SELL A HOUSE OR ANY PIECE OF REAL ESTATE

When your house is on the market and you can't get it to sell, you have to back off a little and realize having control in a situation like this means getting out of the way. This may sound contradictory coming from someone who believes that the mind controls every-thing. There's another aspect to creating what you want that's much more subtle. It has to do with realizing that the universe works *through* you and it can't flow properly if you think it's *you* that everything comes from.

We are all nothing but channels for Spirit, and we've been raised to believe that it's our will that's doing all the work. So, when it comes to selling your house you have to "Let Go and Let God" take care of things. Part of this involves being honest about whether you're happy about leaving the home you're in. Many of us are in conflict about leaving the past behind, so take a good look and see if there's emotional energy tying things up.

The next thing to do is realize that you're a "steward" or an "ele-mental" who's only here to facilitate the process and surrender to playing that role. Part of doing that involves clearing the space. You can start by polishing all the brass on the doorknobs at every entrance to your home. Polish the outside lanterns too.

Next focus on the pathway that leads to the front door. Clean it up and make it as inviting as you can by planting flowers or placing potted plants on the front steps. Hang a wreath of laurel or grapevine laced with strawberries on every door, wash all the windows, and hang crystal prisms up so that rainbows fill the house whenever the sun shines.

Go to the market and stock up on those frozen loaves of bread they sell in the freezer section. While you're at it, pick up a couple of frozen apple or blueberry pies too. Every time the realtor calls and tells you that someone is coming to look at the house, pop a loaf of bread or one of the pies into the oven. People respond subconsciously so well to the smell of hot pastry that whoever's checking out your house can't help but fall in love with it if there's something in the oven when they come. If it's too much trouble to bake all this stuff, you can use potpourri, but the real thing works better and you'll be able to eat it too.

Many people who move a lot (and most realtors) swear by those little plastic Saint Joseph statues. You can pick one up at any Christian or Catholic bookstore. They cost six or seven bucks. When you get it home say a little incantation over it and bury it upside down on your front lawn.

You should do all these things as a matter of course. If you want to get things moving even more quickly, you can add the following spell.

The "Mi Casa, Su Casa" Spell

WHAT YOU'LL NEED

An orange candle to represent you
6 green candles to represent prospective buyers
A gold pillar candle to represent your house
A mirror big enough to place the candles on
Patchouli incense
Musk oil

2 tablespoons each of ground cinnamon, sugar, and ginger
A yard of red satin ribbon
Photos of your house along with any clippings
of the house from the realty ads
A nail
A red pen or marker
Matches

Start this spell when the Moon is new. This will allow your developing idea to grow the same way a plant does. The spell will carry over in its effects until the Moon is full. Day by day, the thoughts you project at the New Moon will increase and magnetically draw your wish to you.

ⓔ ⓔ ⓔ

Gather all of your ingredients, cast a circle, and light the incense. With the nail, inscribe the orange candle with your name and the words, "Fast Luck." Anoint it wick to base with musk oil. Inscribe the green candles with the words "Buyer #1," "Buyer #2," etc., and etch dollar signs ($) all over each candle. Anoint the green candles base to wick with the musk oil.

Now take the big gold candle, inscribe it with the asking price, and carve the word "SOLD!" into it. Anoint the gold candle wick to base with musk oil and roll *all* of the candles in the cinnamon, ginger, and sugar mixture. Arrange the candles on the mirror with the gold one in the center surrounded by the six green candles. Place your candle front and center.

Take the picture and the clippings of the house, write the asking price and the word "SOLD!" on each of them, anoint them with three drops of musk, and kiss them one at a time. Place these under your candle.

Let all your intentions be magnified by the light of the candles glowing in the mirror, and place all of the pictures under the gold candle. After you do this, say the following words out loud seven times:

My house will attract more buyers than I can count,
Clamoring to offer me the desired amount,
For this property and everything that goes with it,
The deal will be sealed in less than a minute!

Now carefully move all of the green candles so that they are right up against the gold one. Tie the red ribbon in a bow around the candles so that they form a bundle. Let everything burn until you feel like you've raised enough energy and when you feel complete, snuff all of the candles out. Leave everything where it is.

In the days following, re-light the candles for a while and recite the incantation above seven times. The phone should start ringing and you'll probably be eating tons of frozen pastry! There *will* be at least one offer by the time the Moon is full. On the night of the Full Moon, bury what remains from this spell in the North corner of your property. If for any reason nothing happens, repeat the spell at the next New Moon.

MOVING RITUAL

The "New Home, New Heart, Fresh Roots, New Start" Ritual

WHAT YOU'LL NEED

Some loose change
An old sugar bowl
1 or 2 cups of dirt
A piece of old lace
2 or 3 pounds of sea salt
Several bunches of fresh or dried chamomile
(use chamomile tea bags if you have to)
4 iron nails or 4 horseshoes
Sage for smudging

When it's time to move, clear out your old place and leave some loose change behind in one of the kitchen drawers. This will bring prosperity to the new owners and ensure luck and prosperity for you too.

Dig up a cup or two of dirt from your old property before you leave town and place it in an old sugar bowl. Wrap this in a piece of lace and treat it like the Holy Grail! When you arrive at your new home on moving day, bury the dirt from the sugar bowl near the front steps of your new house. This will make the transition easier.

Before you move a stick of furniture out of the moving van, fill up a wash bucket with a cup of sea salt and three handfuls of fresh or dried chamomile. Refilling the bucket as necessary, wash all the floors with this "potion." When they are all dry, sweep up any residue left from the dried herbs and toss it out the back door. This will protect your new space from harm, bad influences, or any other form of negativity.

Now take the four nails or four horseshoes and place them with the sharp end pointing out or the curved side pointing in at the four corners of the first floor. This will protect your new space from all harm, bad influences, or any other form of negativity.

Once all of this is done, spark up the sage and let it burn as you unload the moving van and start settling in.

SPELL TO USE WHEN IT'S TIME TO MOVE AND YOU HAVE NO PLACE TO GO

What do you do when the house you're in gets sold and you can't find a new place? What do you do when you wake up one morning and realize you just can't stay where you are one more day and you have no money and nowhere to run? In this type of situation, it's your faith and your connection to Spirit that's being tested. We all know how to be really "Zen" when we're meditating every morning, but being "Zen" when the prospect of landing out on the street is imminent requires more philosophical guts. What you have to call on at a crossroad like this is total trust in the fact that because you are a child of God like the rest of us, the universe will take care of you. The following spell will help you center yourself enough to surrender to whatever the fates have planned for you.

The "Gypsy Lives In All of Us" Spell

WHAT YOU'LL NEED

The "Joker" from a deck of playing cards,
or "The Fool" from a Tarot deck
An orange candle to represent you
Musk oil
Rose incense
2 tablespoons of powdered ginger
2 tablespoons of ground coffee
A piece of tumbled bloodstone
A picture of a house cut from a magazine
An old key
A lodestone or a refrigerator magnet
A piece of parchment or paper cut from a brown paper bag
A pen
A nail
A map of the world or a map of the area you want to live in
4 tablespoons of sea salt
A mirror or a circle of tinfoil 2 feet in diameter
A red bandana
A small trowel or shovel

This is an emergency situation most of the time so any day you want to work on will do in a pinch. If by chance you have a choice, pick a New Moon to do this spell.

℮ ℮ ℮

Gather all of your ingredients together and cast a circle. Light the incense and with the nail, inscribe your name, the Sowelo rune ᛋ, and the words "I love my new place!" into the candle. Anoint the candle wick to base with musk oil. Blend the ginger and the coffee together and roll the candle in this mixture until it fills up all the grooves.

Place the mirror or the sheet of foil down in front of you and set the candle in the center. As you light the candle, slide the "Joker" or "The Fool" underneath it. Sprinkle a circle of salt all around the mirror/foil, starting at the North and moving clockwise.

Now get out the map and the picture that you cut out of the magazine, fold them up together and place them inside the circle. Charge the piece of bloodstone and the key in your left hand with your visions of a safe haven. Once this is done, lay them both on top of the map and anoint everything with musk oil. Place the lodestone or the magnet next to the bloodstone and the key and say these words out loud seven times:

> My spirit is free and I'm floating on air,
> Like a feather I drift without even one care,
> About where I will land or where I might be.
> Great Spirit is taking good care of me!

Snuff out the candle. Take a ride or a walk to any dirt crossroad where there's no traffic and no one around. If you live out in the country, you won't have a problem with this. If you live in the city, you might have to do this part of the spell inside. That's OK. Just mark off an "X" on the floor somewhere. Bring the map, the picture, the bloodstone, the magnet, and the key along with you. Unfold the map and lay it down in the center of the crossroad or the "X". Place everything on top of the map and say the following words out loud three times:

> Spirit come and blow me East or West,
> Blow me North or South if that seems best.

I long for a tranquil, peaceful nest,
Find me a home and put my worries to rest.

Dance around the map three times in a clockwise direction. Bury the key, the magnet, the picture, the map, and the bloodstone at the crossroads or set them on an eastern windowsill.

Every day thereafter re-light the orange candle and let it burn as you get centered and recite *both* of the incantations above three times each. Focus on the fact that just because you don't have a place to run to right *now*, who's to say the next *hour* won't yield good news?

When the candle burns out, wrap the remains in the red bandana along with the map and the other objects, if you didn't bury them. Keep this charm under your pillow and carry "The Joker" or "The Fool" in your wallet to remind you that the universe is taking good care of everything. You'll have a new nest to fly to before you know it. On the day that you move in, bury the charm in the red bandana near the doorstep of your new home.

CHAPTER 8

Money Spells, or Dollars & Sense

One area in which we could all use a little magic is our relationship with money! It doesn't matter if you're rich or poor. Everyone has money issues. In the last twenty or thirty years, so many books on prosperity and abundance have been published that we *should* have it all figured out by now, but we don't. I won't even pretend to know what's going on with money because I figure out where I'm at with it on a day-to-day basis. But I do know something about manifesting cash when I need it.

I have friends who have always had a lot of money and what I see is that it's a lot harder to go from having it to not having any. They're so accustomed to being able to have whatever they want it's really scary to them when there's nothing in the bank. Nothing in the bank is par for the course at my house. I've learned that just because I don't have money today doesn't mean I won't have it tomorrow. I know how to manifest what I need and am getting better at creating resources all the time.

It may be hard for you to have faith in money spells written by a witch who's broke (by other people's standards), but I'm here to tell you that even when I *am* broke, I feel rich because I know that I am totally supported by the Universe. I'd rather have health, faith, love, friendship, and serenity than all the money in the world. That's real wealth if you ask me. *But,* there are times when it takes money to get where you want to go. The spells in this chapter will help you manifest the green stuff when you need it.

SPELLS TO MANIFEST CASH WHEN YOU HAVE NONE

This spell is for those times when you haven't got two cents to rub together.

The "Money Potion" Spell

WHAT YOU'LL NEED

An orange taper candle
A 2-quart saucepan and
a wooden stirring spoon
A quart of spring water
A quart-sized jar
Matches
A nail
A magnet or a lodestone
3 tablespoons ground cinnamon or 3 cinnamon sticks
3 tablespoons ground cloves
1 tablespoon allspice
3 chestnuts
A pine bough
Cinnamon oil
Musk oil
A dollar bill and 10 pennies
A piece of parchment or paper cut from a brown paper bag
A pen

Do this spell when the Moon is waxing on a Thursday, a Friday, or a Sunday. The waxing rays of the Moon cause everything to increase and get bigger. I like Thursdays because they're ruled by Jupiter–the planet of wealth and abundance. This is the all time best day to do *any* spell that involves increasing your cash flow. Fridays are ruled by Venus and since Venus has as much to say about our cash flow as it does about our love life, Fridays are the next best day to do a money spell on. Since Sundays are ruled by the Sun and the Sun is the most positive all around influence, there's nothing wrong with working a money spell on a Sunday.

ℰ ℰ ℰ

You'll be working in your kitchen, so cast a circle around the stove as best you can. Gather all of your ingredients. With the nail, inscribe the candle with dollar signs and the words "Fast Luck and Success." Anoint it wick to base with the cinnamon and musk oils. Take a little of the spices you'll be using and rub them into the candle too. Light the candle and set it to burn near the stove.

Keep the jar nearby while you mix up your potion. Pour the spring water into the saucepan and turn on the stove. As you bring the water to a boil, start adding the cinnamon, cloves, and allspice. Add three drops of musk oil and four drops of cinnamon oil to the pot.

Charge the magnet in your left hand with the thought that you're a magnet for money. Do the same thing with the chestnuts and toss them and the magnet into the potion.

Hold the dollar bill and the coins in your left hand and as you do this visualize them multiplying over and over again. Toss them into the pot along with everything else.

As this brew starts to boil, turn it down and let it simmer, stirring it with the pine bough. As you do this, say these words out loud over and over again:

> *Money and good checks, possessions in great measure,*
> *My pockets, purse, and home all filled up with treasure.*
> *Wealth and riches fly to me,*
> *Whatever I want comes immediately.*

Keep stirring what's in the pot and take in the aroma of this potion with every breath. Turn the flame on the stove down as low as it will go. Sit at the table and write down on paper *exactly* what you want to manifest financially. When you're done, read it out loud. Put three drops each of musk and cinnamon oil onto this wish list, fold it up, kiss it once, and pop it into the potion.

Keep stirring everything with the pine bough until you feel clear that all your intentions will manifest. Let the mixture cool a little and pour all of it into the jar. Cap the jar and move it to the kitchen table along with the orange candle.

Sit there for a few minutes and finish the spell by repeating the incantation above three more times. When you are complete, snuff out the candle.

Leave it where it is and burn it for a little while every day until it's gone. Bury the remains in the East where the Sun rises. Dab the potion on your wallet, your checkbook, your credit cards, and yourself. Every time you write a check, dab some on. Sprinkle it on your money so that the Wiccan law, "What you send out comes back to thee" will reign in your financial world!

What goes around comes around, so bottle it up, give some to your friends, and *always* carry a little vial of it in your purse.

ANOTHER SPELL TO TURN THE FINANCIAL TIDE WHEN IT'S OUT

The "Manna From Heaven" Spell

WHAT YOU'LL NEED

7 green candles
An orange candle
A nail
Cinnamon and musk oil
A mirror to set up your candles on
3 tablespoons each cinnamon, cloves, allspice, and basil

3 tablespoons sea salt
Cinnamon, musk, or sandalwood incense
All the money and change you can find in the house
A piece of parchment or paper cut from a brown paper bag
A pen
A magnet

--- --- --- --- --- --- --- --- --- ---

Choose a Thursday, a Friday, or a Sunday under a waxing Moon to do this spell. (See the "Money Potion" spell on p. 110 for an explanation.)

ⓔ ⓔ ⓔ

Cast a circle and light the incense. Inscribe all seven of the green candles with dollar signs and the Fehu rune ᚠ. With the nail, inscribe the orange candle with dollar signs and the words "Instant Success." Anoint all the candles wick to base with both the musk and the cinnamon oil and rub the spices into the inscriptions.

Set the green candles up in a circle on the mirror in front of you and light them, using the first one to light the second one, the second one to light the third one, and so on.

Take all the money and change you have found in the house and arrange it in a "wreath" around the circle of candles.

Now mix the sea salt with the spices in a mortar and pestle and as you do chant these words out loud:

> Bless this money and bring me more,
> I have plenty, more than ever before.
> No more worry and no more trouble,
> Money come to me, on the double!

Sprinkle the salt and spices over the circle of money. Now set the orange candle in the center of the circle of green candles. Don't light it yet.

Write down on the paper exactly what you want. When you're done, charge the magnet with your intentions in your left hand and run it over the words you've written. Put three drops of musk oil and three drops of cinnamon oil on the paper. Kiss it once to give it life and slide it under the orange candle. Place the magnet next to the orange candle. Light this candle and sit here for as long as you like, focused on your wish. When you feel complete, snuff out all the candles in the order they were lit and leave everything where it is.

Every day, re-light the candles in the same way and repeat the incantation. When you're done, snuff everything out. When all of the candles are burned down to nothing, bury them in the East along with the paper and the magnet. Keep the money in a bowl on the windowsill until the Moon is full. On the day of the Full Moon, take a dollar, a quarter, a nickel, and a penny from the bowl and give it to the first person you see.

MONEY CHARMS

Sometimes I can't be bothered doing a spell. This is when charms can come in handy. You carry them with you everywhere and they serve as a constant reminder of your intention–in this case, to manifest more money. Even if you make a charm and leave it on your kitchen windowsill, every time you wash the dishes or walk by it, you'll be reminded. They also make wonderful, off-the-wall little gifts.

The Chestnut Charm

WHAT YOU'LL NEED
_____

A chestnut
A dollar bill

I think this one's really old. My friend Sue turned me on to it. Take a chestnut and a dollar bill and charge them with your intentions in your left hand. Don't worry about whether you're doing it right. Take my word for it: your thoughts get channeled right into whatever you're holding in your hand. Wrap the dollar bill around the chestnut and carry it with you in your pocket or purse. That's all there is to it. Wouldn't it be great if they gave these away as favors at baby and wedding showers instead of those little plastic baskets of Jordan Almonds?

The "Seaweed Cocktail" Charm

WHAT YOU'LL NEED

Seaweed, dulse, or kelp
Widemouthed jar
Whiskey

You know those pretty jars of herbed vinegars people keep around for decorative purposes? This charm is sort of like that. It's an oldie but goodie that will help you maintain a constant flow of steady cash. For best results whip this up when the Moon is full. Go to the seashore and gather some seaweed. If you don't live near the ocean, just go to the health food store and buy some dulse or kelp. Find a jar that has a wide-mouth opening and stuff it full with the seaweed. If you have a green or red glass jar, it'll be more effective. Yellow works too. Pour enough whiskey over the seaweed to cover it completely. Seal the jar and keep it on your windowsill.

The "Ginger Root" Charm

WHAT YOU'LL NEED

3 pieces of ginger root
10 copper pennies
Red kerchief (if winter)

A week or so before the Moon gets full, go buy three good-sized pieces of ginger root and sleep with them under your pillow. On the night of the Full Moon, charge each root with prosperous intentions, one at a time, in your left hand. When this charging is complete, bury all three roots in the ground along with ten copper pennies. If it's winter, wrap the ginger roots and the pennies in a red kerchief and stash the charm in the East end of the cellar.

A LITTLE SPELL FOR THOSE OF YOU WITH MORE "GOTHIC" TASTE

The "Food for the Spirit" Spell

WHAT YOU'LL NEED

1 green candle
A nail
Musk oil
Moss from a gravestone
1 whole chestnut, walnut, peanut, or hazelnut
A good steak

This dicey old spell has a lot of kick to it. If you're a vegetarian, you'll probably want to skip it. There's meat involved.

Start preparing this one when the Moon is new. You're going to want those waxing lunar forces working in your favor. Over the next two weeks as the Moon grows in fullness, your money situation will improve and increase right along with it.

☙ ☙ ☙

With the nail, inscribe the green candle with dollar signs and anoint it with musk oil. Now roll the candle in the gravestone moss. You probably have some in the cupboard, but if you don't, you know where to find it! Let this candle burn for a little while each day and as it does sit staring into the flame and think wealthy thoughts.

When the candle burns down to a puddle of wax, plop a whole chestnut, walnut, peanut, or a hazelnut into the wax and roll it all up into a ball. On the day that the Moon gets full, go out and buy a really nice steak. After dark, go to the nearest graveyard and bury the wax ball near one of the graves. Leave the meat to mark the spot where you buried the charm. As you walk away from the gravestone, don't look back and say these words out loud:

> *Spirits who wander and watch over all,*
> *You've got time on your hands so hear my call.*
> *The feast I offer you will feed your pleasure,*
> *Work your magic to bring me treasure.*

Let the forces of serendipity take it from here. When you get home from this nocturnal outing, draw a sea salt bath and burn some sage just to make sure you're clear of any astral forces that may have decided they needed company.

SPELL TO GET BACK MONEY THAT'S OWED YOU

If you're owed money, you know what a hassle it can be getting people to pay you back. This is a particularly good spell to use if you own rental property and have tenants who are behind on the rent. If your situation is complicated by a host of other factors such as a messy divorce, a split with your honey, or bad judgment on your part, proceed with caution and tell the truth.

If the money situation has got you in court and you're going for the throat, remember that karmic law needs to be respected. What you think is rightfully yours *may* not be, so be honest with yourself and have integrity in everything you do.

The "It's About Time" Spell

A green candle to represent the person who owes you money
A white candle to represent you
Musk incense
Musk oil
A nail
1 tablespoon each cinnamon and nutmeg
The contents of a bag of Earl Grey tea
A refrigerator magnet or a lodestone
A dollar bill and some loose change

The Full Moon is best for this one as you want the maximum impact in these situations. The Full Moon will definitely help who-ever owes you money to wake up and smell the coffee.

℮ ℮ ℮

Cast a circle if you wish and light your incense. With the nail, inscribe the green candle with the name of the person who's indebted to you. Along with his or her name write, "It's time to pay [your name here] back what I owe her." Anoint it base to wick with the musk oil. Roll the candle in the cinnamon and nutmeg.

On the white candle inscribe your name and the words, "I am a magnet for all the money that is owed me." A few dollar signs will help too, if you have room. Anoint the candle, wick to base with the musk oil and roll it in the spices.

Place the green candle to the left and put the white candle to the right. Take all the loose change and pile it up around the green can-dle. Place the magnet next to the white candle. Starting at the green candle, sprinkle a "prosperity trail" between the two candles with the Earl Grey tea. When this is done say these words out loud:

Whenever [the indebted one] thinks of me,
The money he/she owes me is all he/she sees.
This magnet will open his/her pockets and purse,
Every dollar comes to me as I say this verse.

Keep repeating the words to this spell as you take the magnet and pick up the change, one coin at a time, and move it from the green candle to the white candle. When all the money is around the white candle, set the magnet down next to it and focus your thoughts on the person who owes you money. Envision them writing you a check, putting cash in an envelope, or writing you a money order. When the vision is clear, snuff the candles out and let them sit where they are.

Spend some time burning them each day and focus your intentions by repeating the incantation. When the candles are all burned down, bury them in the North along with the change. You should have your money back by the New Moon, if not sooner.

SPELLS AND CHARMS TO DRAW CUSTOMERS TO YOUR BUSINESS

Those of us who are in business for ourselves often feel vulnerable to fluctuations in the market. The following rituals are more like little "tricks" or superstitions that work to bring customers with money to spend into your life. Anyone can benefit from them, so even if you're not in the business world, you can try them at home. Whoever shows up at your door will come to give you money or hook you up with opportunities that will make you more prosperous. For best results do these rituals once a month at the New or Full Moon.

The "Abundance Floor Wash" Ritual

WHAT YOU'LL NEED:

Sea salt
Epsom salts

A large jar
Fresh or dried spearmint, chamomile, and basil (a handful each)
Green food coloring

On the day of the Full Moon, mix four parts sea salt with one part Epsom salts in a large jar. Add a handful each of fresh or dried spearmint, chamomile, and basil and enough green food coloring to color the salts without dissolving them. Shake well. Sprinkle this on the floor of your shop or business and sweep it all up and out the door. This will clear the space and draw a steady flow of customers to your business.

If you're feeling industrious, you can mix the herbed salts in a bucket of hot water and wash more luck and business into your life. Either way. I've used this many times and seen it produce results immediately.

The "Pesto, Pennies, And Prosperity" Charm

WHAT YOU'LL NEED

Handfuls of dried basil or loose change
Doormat

Sprinkle three or four handfuls of fresh or dried basil under the doormat at the entrance to your business to draw in customers. You can do the same thing with pennies, nickels, dimes, and quarters. Any amount of loose change scattered under the doormat is good for abundance. You don't necessarily have to turn this into a ritual. It's something any good crone should do as a matter of course. It wouldn't hurt to do it right before the Full Moon and you can keep the flow coming by changing the basil and the coins once a month.

Red Doors

I learned a long time ago that if you paint the front door to your home or business red it will give you a financial boost. Don't take my word for it. Drive around your town and notice whose got red doors. I'm willing to bet they're the ones with all the money.

A Charm Bag For Steady Cash

Charm bags are great because they're portable. If you keep them on your body, or nearby, in your purse or briefcase, the energy they generate vibrates in your auric field all the time and makes you a magnet for the forces you're trying to attract. You can also hide or bury them anywhere if it suits your purposes.

I use this one all the time. If you have your own business, keep it tucked in your cash register or your cash box. You can carry it in your purse, or hang it from the rear view mirror of your car, too.

WHAT YOU'LL NEED:

A small gold lamé or green satin pouch
3 tonka beans (they sound exotic but you can get them at a good health food store or craft store)
3 marigold buds
1 cinnamon stick
A piece of tumbled citrine
10 pennies
A magnet

Whip this up just before the Full Moon or on a Thursday or Friday when the Moon is waxing. The energy right before the Full Moon is packed with magnetic, attractive forces that will pull the green stuff right to you. If you're too busy to do this at that time, then use any Thursday or Friday as the Moon waxes to make this charm. Both days vibrate on the same wavelength that money and abundance flow on. Those frequencies will get transferred into your charm.

@ @ @

A circle isn't necessary as long as you're intentions are sharp and clear. Gather all your ingredients together on a table in front of you and charge them, one at a time, in your left hand with thoughts of steady cash. Pop them all into the pouch and say these words out loud:

Riches and wealth fly to me now,
I have money to spare and always know how
To bring mountains of cash and good checks by the score.
This bag is a magnet that attracts even more.

You're all set! Keep this wherever you think it will do the most good.

ANOTHER GOOD MONEY SPELL THAT STRENGTHENS OVER TIME

I find that it's easy to get money flowing in quickly; the hard part can be keeping it coming after the initial blast of spell work. This spell helps the energy you put out grow and strengthen over time.

The "Seeds of Wealth and Prosperity" Spell

WHAT YOU'LL NEED

A green, yellow, or gold candle
Musk oil
Musk incense
Ground cloves
A nail

3 beans, any kind (lima beans work best)
3 big handfuls of red clover
(use fresh or get it dried at the health food store)
A piece of parchment or paper cut from a brown paper bag
A pen

A waxing Moon and a Thursday or a Friday will work best for this spell. Notice that you'll be planting the beans. Symbolically, this will cause your resources to grow and continue to flow. Any good gardener knows that things grow better if they're planted between the New and Full Moon. Thursdays and Fridays are the most benefic days of the week and perfect for financial work of any kind.

ⓔ ⓔ ⓔ

A circle is optional. Do what feels right. Light your incense and with the nail, inscribe your candle with symbols of wealth and prosperity. Dollar signs are the old standby, but be inventive and use your own imagery. Anoint the candle wick to base with the musk oil and roll it in the ground cloves. Set it in front of you and light it.

Around this candle, spread a circle of clover, always remembering to move in a clockwise direction.

With your pen and paper, write down exactly what you want to manifest in a dollar amount. Don't limit yourself in any way. Slide this paper under the candle. As you sit facing the candle flame, hold the beans in your left hand and say these words out loud seven times:

> I am blessed with riches, coins and money,
> My wealth increases every day.
> The seeds I hold will bring me milk and honey,
> What sprouts tonight will pay my way.

Charge the beans with the idea that they are investments that will grow and provide a continuous return. Walk to the front door of your house and plant the beans in the ground or in a flowerpot in the North corner of your property.

When you're done planting the seeds, return to the house and snuff out the candle. Leave everything where it is and light the candle for an hour or so a day until it burns out. At the next New Moon, bury the remains of the candle along with the clover and the note where you planted the seeds.

CHAPTER 9

Old Girls at Work: Spells for Creating and Keeping the Perfect Job

By the time we reach menopause, the joys of love, the domestic urges, and the need to be a caretaker often become less interesting to us than our careers. This is natural because all that stuff that we do when we're younger gets old after awhile and it's more exciting being out there in the world having an impact and being creative in a different way.

For those of us who spent the first half of our lives pouring every ounce of our being into our homes, our relationships, and our families, it's often not until we reach menopause that we take our first peek into the world of work and career. Not the case for me, but I certainly know lots of women who've been down this road. They hit fifty and all of a sudden the world opens up and they're given the opportunity to dedicate all of who they are to something that's actually their own for the first time. This can be frightening sometimes, but more often than not it's exhilarating to finally be free to go out and get a life. There's "No keeping you down on the farm after you've seen Paree!" and it's always amusing to watch those close to us do double takes as we fly out the door on winged feet and go off to work at what we love.

We old girls get more powerful once we pass menopause, and it's a hell of a lot easier to make things happen than it was when we were younger and had no clue that we were more than just a pretty face. But the fact that we're more empowered can cause problems. The world is still so geared to the old patriarchal mind-set that when a fifty plus female dynamo shows up at the office, people don't know what hit them. Who knew that all the years we spent raising kids and sublimating our energy were basically boot camp or a form of preparation for what we *really* got put on the planet to do.

For those of us who have been in career mode all our lives the situation appears to be different, but it's not really. If you have been schlepping off to work for thirty years, you may be getting ready to retire or debating whether or not to stick it out where you are until you can collect all those retirement benefits. Anyone who is ready to leave the workplace has to adjust to a different way of being with themselves. Most of us have plenty of ideas and enthusiasm about what to do with our lives now that we're free and we're raring to go. It's not a problem.

For those of you who are a few years shy of cashing in on your 401K and all the other good things that are coming to you, the choice is harder. My advice to anyone in this situation is, follow your heart. Spending your precious time forcing yourself to do something you hate because in your mind you think your future security depends on it will eventually make you sick and render it impossible to do anything but pay the doctor with all those benefits. Real security has nothing to do with your job. It comes from within.

I'm including the following spells to help you cope with and be creative about the different positions you find yourself in relative to the work place. Before you do *any* of them, give yourself a good pep talk and remember that you're way more powerful than that twenty-six year old who simply hasn't lived long enough to develop the wisdom and compassion that only come with time and a few wrinkles.

SPELL TO HELP YOU GET THE JOB THAT YOU REALLY, REALLY WANT

There are a lot of situations where this spell will come in handy. It'll help you if you're embarking on a career for the first time, but it's also a good one to use if you're in a job that's less than pleasant and you're summoning up the courage to go after a new position that's more challenging and satisfying.

The "God, I Want This Job" Spell

WHAT YOU'LL NEED

A gold candle to represent you
A pink candle to represent the person who will interview you
Rose incense
Rose oil
Rosemary oil
Lavender oil
2 good healthy handfuls of marigold blossoms
Powdered ginger
2 pieces of ginger root
Powdered mace
A circle of tinfoil 2 feet in diameter
A yard of red rattail cord
A piece of parchment or paper cut from a brown paper bag
A pen
A nail

Do this spell on the night of the Full Moon. Spells like this require the maximum punch and the Full Moon will infuse your work with the best possible vibrations.

℮ ℮ ℮

You'll want to cast a circle. Before you cast your circle fill up the bathtub with hot water. Toss in half of the marigolds along with one ginger root and ten drops of rosemary oil. Hop in and take a nice long bath. Bathing in marigold water brings you the admiration of everyone you meet. The piece of ginger root will insure total success.

Rosemary oil is good for everything, but I'm using it here because it gives women power and makes them strong.

After you're done, be sure to save the bath ingredients. You'll be using them later. Gather all your other ingredients and cast your circle. You'll give this spell more kick if you work naked, but that's up to you. Light the rose incense and with the nail, inscribe your name into the gold candle along with the Teiwaz rune ↑. Anoint the candle wick to base with rose oil and roll it in the powdered ginger. Inscribe the pink candle with the name and/or title of the person who will be interviewing you and anoint it base to wick with the lavender oil. Then roll the pink candle in the powdered mace.

Place the circular sheet of tinfoil down in front of you and draw the Gebo rune ✕, being careful not to cut through the surface of the foil. Gebo is the symbol that I use when a spell involves the need to bring two parties together in unison. Place the gold candle on the foil in the left hand section of the "✕". Place the pink candle in the right hand section of the "✕". Light them both from the same match.

Now take the piece of red rattail cord and lay it around the circle of foil. With everything set and the candles glowing, write on the piece of parchment or paper exactly what it is that you wish to happen in your own words, visualizing clearly how you want the interview to go. When you're done, lay the parchment in the center of the foil right where the "✕" crosses. Now say the following words out loud seven times:

> I am the beautiful shining one,
> My aura glows as bright as the Sun.
> When (Name of the person who will interview you)
>   sees my face,
> They will know in their heart that I've won the race.
> It feels good to know that I'll have work that's steady,
> The job I want is mine already.

After you've finished this incantation, tie the rattail cord in a loose bow and sit as long as you want to, conjuring up visions of success and fulfillment. When you feel complete, snuff out the candles and leave everything where it is.

Every day, for a little while, re-light the candles and recite the words above three times. When everything is burned down to nothing, wrap up in the foil the remains of the candles along with the marigold blossoms and the ginger root from the ritual bath and tie everything up with the red rattail cord.

On the day that you go for your interview, take another bath with marigold flowers, the other piece of ginger root, and ten more drops of rosemary oil. When you're all dressed and ready to go, remember to bring the tinfoil charm with you in your purse. Don't worry about a thing. This is a "kick-ass" spell. It works every time.

SPELL TO KEEP A JOB THAT
APPEARS TO BE SLIPPING AWAY

Most of us panic when there's a vibe at work that makes it seem as if we're about to get canned. We have been raised to believe that our security and all of our prosperity comes from our job. It's been true all along but only recently rediscovered that our abundance actually comes from within. What do you know! We source it! It's hard to believe but more of us are "getting" all the time that not only are we *not* our jobs, we don't *need* them if they don't serve our highest interests. If you sense that you're about to get laid off, it just *may* be because your Higher Self knows that you have better things to do. The old cliché, "When one door closes another one opens" has a lot of truth to it.

Before you do the spell that follows, check in with the wise forces of the universe. Get a piece of string about a foot long and loop it around a paper clip. On a piece of paper write "The impending layoff is in my highest good." Hold the string with the paper clip over this statement and wait for it to move. If it moves up and down, you know that it's in your soul's best interests to move on to something new and there's no need to do the spell. If the string moves side to side, you know that it's better for you to do whatever you can to hold on to your position. In that case, use the following spell.

The "Don't Lay Me Off" Spell

A bag of pecans in the shell
A red bandana
Musk oil

Any day of the week but Tuesday or Saturday will work for this spell, as long as the Moon is waxing. The Mars vibration that rules Tuesdays is a little too contentious to be of any help in a spell like this and Saturday is a definite "no-no". When you're worried about keeping your job, the Saturnine vibration that rules Saturdays would probably make things take a turn for the worse.

℮ ℮ ℮

On a day when the Moon is waxing, go buy a bag of pecans in the shell. Start eating the nuts one at a time and save the shells. When you're done eating the nutmeats, wrap all of the shells in the red bandana and tie it tight. Anoint this charm with seven drops of musk oil and hide it somewhere in your workplace where no one will find it. Things will shift magically at work and your tension and paranoia will subside.

If the same energy starts to build again, repeat the spell with a new bag of nuts and a new bandana and replace the old charm with a new one.

SPELL TO CREATE THE PERFECT JOB

Many of us work because we have to and we do things on a daily basis that take us far away from who we really are. We've been educated to believe that "that's life!" and that everyone has to put their ideals aside in order to pay the piper, the landlord, and the electric company. It would be wonderful if people knew enough to raise their kids with the idea that the greatest thing about being human is that you can have whatever you want, as long as you know what it is. Unfortunately, that wasn't what was happening when our parents were "Baby Booming"!

I've seen so many women who are incredibly talented, creative, and intelligent fritter all that valuable energy away punching in and out every day for a paycheck. It's funny how we all believe that if we just keep working harder and put more time in eventually we'll be able to do what we love. Look around. The people who are working the hardest are getting nowhere, and the ones who aren't are somewhere having a ball with little or no effort. We got sold a bill of goods. The mind controls everything that happens in our lives.

If there's a huge gap between what you know you want and what you're doing every day, use the following spell. If you're one of those women who's putting off doing what you really love until after you retire, this spell is perfect for you! Remember, waiting for your ship to come in is a big gamble. If you're not joyful about what you do every day, you'll get so old, sour, and sick you'll never be able to attract the abundance you want.

The "I Believe I Can Have What I Want, Including the Perfect Job" Spell

WHAT YOU'LL NEED

A gold candle to represent you
A mirror or a piece of foil about 2 feet-square
Patchouli oil
Musk incense
2 tablespoons of powdered ginger
4 tablespoons of sea salt
2 pieces of parchment or paper cut from a brown paper bag
A pen
A nail
Pictures from magazines or photographs
that embody what you see yourself doing

A lodestone or a refrigerator magnet
A metal bowl and a fireproof trivet
Matches
A small jar with a lid

————————————————

Start this spell when the Moon is new. If you're doing this spell, the whole idea that you can have whatever you want is a new concept that you're creating in your head. You're going to need the new-ness of the New Moon to match the energy you're generating. The idea, and the belief that it is true, will grow as the Moon waxes to fullness.

ⓔ ⓔ ⓔ

Gather all your ingredients and cast a circle. Light the incense and with the nail, inscribe the candle with your name and the Teiwaz rune ↑. You will also want to inscribe the symbol for the planets Mars and Jupiter on this candle (see Important Stuff to Know, II).

Anoint the candle wick to base with patchouli oil and roll it in the powdered ginger. Lay the mirror or the sheet of foil down in front of you, place the candle in the middle, and light the candle. Sprinkle the sea salt all around the mirror/foil in a circle. Start at the North and move clockwise.

As you let this candle burn, write on the first sheet of parchment all the feelings and fears you have about the job you have now. Place this to the left of the circle of salt, making sure to keep it outside of the circle. On the second piece of parchment, write down everything you're thinking and feeling about what you could be doing, want to do, or imagine you could do. Don't hold back. Remember, all things are possible!

Draw the lodestone or magnet over every word you've written, anoint the paper with three drops of patchouli oil, kiss it once, and place it inside the salt circle underneath the gold candle. If you have any pictures of your dreams, anoint them with patchouli, kiss them once, and place them inside the circle also.

Lay the lodestone or magnet on top of the pictures and/or the parchment and let the energy build as your dreams begin to manifest. As you visualize what you want, say these words out loud seven times:

> *I am free of all doubt about what's possible in my life,*
> *As of this moment I release every fear.*
> *Now that I know I can have what I want,*
> *The old path is gone and the new path is clear.*

After you've recited the above incantation, burn the piece of parchment that has all your feelings and fears about the job you're currently attached to in the metal bowl. When it burns out completely, put the ashes inside the jar.

With your old beliefs about what's true safely bottled, sit for a while and soak in the dreams that are coming to life inside the circle. See yourself doing what you love and being paid well for it.

When you feel complete, snuff out the gold candle and leave the circle intact. Take the bottle with the ashes of your old attitude in it, hop in your car and drive West, to the next town if possible. Find a secluded spot to bury the bottle. Once it's in the ground point to the spot and say:

> *I no longer need to be a slave,*
> *It's time to live the life I crave.*

Just for the hell of it, it might be good to add:

> *In no way will this spell reverse or cast upon me*
> *any curse.*

Every day thereafter, re-light the candle and activate the visions that are brewing in your mind and heart. Sit for a period of time feeding these thoughts.

On a night just before the Moon is full, take the remains of the candle, the salt sweepings, and the magnet and wrap them inside the parchment and the pictures. Bury this charm in the North and let Mother Earth receive your dreams and help you manifest them. Changes should start happening right away so pay attention and don't take anything for granted.

Good luck with your new life. You'll kick yourself for not doing this sooner, but better late than never!

SPELL TO EASE THE STRESS OF DEALING WITH A BOSS OR CO-WORKER WHO'S A TOTAL JERK

The ins and outs of dealing with neurotic bosses, their idiosyncrasies, and their unresolved childhood issues take up a lot of energy. We've all been through this one! I spent years working for people who were far less intelligent and gifted than I was. It's so hard to be subservient to someone when you know you have more integrity in your little finger than they'll ever have in this life or the next! When the pressure gets to be too much, use this spell. It works just as well on coworkers and associates who make the job scene less than pleasant.

The "Get Out of My Face and Just Let Me Do My Job" Spell

WHAT YOU'LL NEED

A poppet (see Chapter 4, p. 42)
made out of pink cloth and stuffed with chamomile
(empty out chamomile tea bags if you have to)
3 feet of black rattail cord
A red candle to represent you
Lavender oil
4 tablespoons of sea salt
A pint-sized jar
A nail

A pen or a needle and thread
Matches

— ·· — ·· — ·· — ·· — ·· — ·· — ·· —

This spell should be done when the Moon is waning. Remember, you're trying to banish the negative influence of someone who is driving you nuts and the waning force of the Moon is perfect for making any type of problem disappear. If you really want to go for it, do this on a Saturday. Saturdays are ruled by the restricting and binding influence of Saturn. The "double whammy" of the waning Moon and the Saturday will render the aggravating person powerless and limit his or her ability to make you insane.

@ @ @

Gather all your ingredients and cast a circle. Have a poppet ready to go. Write, or better yet embroider, the name of the person whose influence you are trying to neutralize on the front of the doll. With the nail, inscribe your name into the red candle and anoint it wick to base with the lavender oil. Light the candle and set it up in front of you. Anoint the poppet with three drops of lavender oil and place it about two feet to the left of the candle. Sprinkle a circle of salt around the candle starting at the North and moving clockwise. This symbolically seals you off and protects you.

Take the poppet in your hand and bind it around and around with the black rattail cord. As you do this, repeat the following words out loud seven times:

> You no longer have the power to influence me
> Your energy is bound by this rope.
> Every time you try to get in my face,
> Something will tell you there's no hope
> Of ever driving me crazy again.
> Thank God, now at last I can cope!

When the image doll is bound up completely, tie it tight, put it inside the jar, and screw on the lid. Drip some of the wax from the red candle over the lid just to be sure that things are airtight. Place the jar behind you and sit for a while with the candle burning, imagining what it will be like to work without any interference from this person. When this vision is clear snuff out the candle and leave everything where it is.

You can do one of several things with the jar. If you think you can safely store it at work, keep it there hidden in your desk somewhere. This could be dangerous, so it might be better to bury it in the West. Another option with this type of spell is to tie the jar to a tree branch and leave it there. I kind of like this idea for its symbolic value. After all, people like this are "for the birds!"

Every night thereafter, re-light the candle and repeat the words written above three times. By or before the New Moon everything should be burned down to a pile of wax. Bury what's left of the candle along with the salt sweepings in the North.

SPELL TO HELP YOU
AMPLIFY THE IMPACT OF YOUR RESUME

Sending out your resume is always a big deal. Nowadays even the stupidest jobs require them. I think people just like to make you nervous or give you the feeling that you're really lucky to be working in retail! Of course, I'm being facetious. Some jobs are totally great and it really does matter to us whether we get them or not. When that's the case, use this spell.

The "Hey, This is Important To Me, Please Pay Attention" Spell

WHAT YOU'LL NEED

All the copies of your resume and
an equal number of addressed envelopes

A purple candle to represent you
Musk incense
Musk oil
2 tablespoons of ginger powder
As many fresh green pine needles as you have envelopes
A mirror or a circle of foil 2 feet in diameter
4 tablespoons of sea salt
A nail
Matches

—··—··—··—··—··—··—··—··—··—

Do this spell any time during the waxing lunar phase. In this kind of work, you need to muster every ounce of magnetic force, and the waxing Moon will be just the ticket. The New Moon, the sixth day after the New Moon, and the day of the Full Moon have the "highest octane", but any time during that two-week period will do just fine.

℮ ℮ ℮

Gather your ingredients and cast a circle. Light the incense. With the nail, inscribe your name and the words "Total Success" on the purple candle. Anoint the candle wick to base with the musk oil and roll it in the ginger powder.

Place the mirror or the foil in front of you. Set the candle in the middle of the mirror/foil and lay all the copies of your resume around it. Put the envelopes there too. Sprinkle a circle of sea salt around the mirror/foil starting at the North and moving clockwise.

In your left hand, charge all of the pine needles with your most positive thoughts, and as you do so, say these words out loud three times:

I call on the power of Mercury's light
To give strength to the spell that I'm working tonight.

May whoever reads the papers I'm sending
Be impressed and awed with respect never ending.
The papers that lie here will convince any and all
To rush to the phone and give me a call,
Just to tell me they want me to take this position,
And allow me to accept their proposition!
So mote it be!

When you've finished chanting this rhyme, tuck one pine nee-dle into the crease of each envelope and put your resume in there too. Seal all the envelopes and leave them in the circle overnight. Snuff out the candle.

The next morning, re-light the candle and wave each envelope over the flame being careful not to scorch or burn anything. Snuff the candle when you're done, leave the circle where it is, and head for the post office.

After you pop your resume in the mail, bide your time. Place your telephone inside the circle with the candle. Light the candle every day thereafter and repeat the words written above as many times as you want to. Let them be your Mantra! The phone will ring within a week and when it does, you'll know you're a witch, just like the rest of us!

SPELL TO USE WHEN IT'S TIME FOR A RAISE

Asking for more money is a real test of your self-worth. It's always a hard thing to do. We often put it off because we're so afraid our boss will say "no!" It's more often the case that your boss *knows* you deserve more money but doesn't know enough to just give it to you. It's a game, and if you realize that, you can play with the idea instead of being intimidated or afraid. Hiding your light under a bushel isn't going to pay the rent, so when you're pumped up enough to take the big risk, use the following spell.

The "Money Isn't Everything But It Sure Would Help To Get Paid More" Spell

A red candle to represent you
A blank check
A green candle to represent
your boss or company
Rose oil
Musk oil
Musk incense
2 to 3 feet of red rattail cord
20.6 inches (the Sacred Cubit) of green satin ribbon
3 tablespoons of cinnamon and sugar
3 tablespoons of salt
A mirror or a circle of foil 2 feet in diameter
A nail

Do this spell when the Moon is waxing. The increasing light of the waxing Moon will increase your paycheck or salary.

℮ ℮ ℮

Gather all your ingredients and cast a circle. Spark up your incense. With the nail, inscribe your name and the words "I am worth all this and more" along with the Teiwaz rune ↑ into the red candle. Anoint the candle wick to base with the musk oil and roll it in the cinnamon and sugar.

Lay the mirror or the sheet of foil down in front of you, set the red candle on it to the left and light it. Carve your boss's name or the name of the company you work for into the green candle and inscribe the words, "Money is no object" on the candle. Anoint this candle base to wick with the rose oil and roll it in what's left of the cinnamon and sugar. Place the green candle on the mirror/foil to the right and light it. Surround the mirror with the red rattail cord and lay the piece of green satin ribbon on the mirror/foil so that it touches the base of both candles. Sprinkle a circle of salt around the mirror/foil.

Now write out the check for the amount you want your wage/salary increase to be and sign your boss's/company's name on it. Place this check underneath the green candle. Meditate for a few minutes on the idea of your boss being overjoyed at the idea of paying you more.

Anoint the green satin ribbon with seven drops of musk oil starting at the green candle and moving one drop at a time toward the red candle. After you've done this say the following words out loud seven times:

It's been a while and now you know
How much I'm worth, and in order to demonstrate
All of your praise,
You'll gladly say 'yes!' when I ask for a raise!"

Each time you repeat the above rhyme, move the check closer to the red candle. By the time you reach the seventh repetition the check should be under your candle.

Pick up the red rattail cord and begin tying nine knots in it. As you tie the first knot say, "By the knot of one, the spell is begun." As you tie the second say, "By the knot of two, it cometh true." As you tie the third say, "By the knot of three, so mote it be!" As you tie the fourth say, "By the knot of four it strengthens more." As you tie the fifth say, "By the knot of five, thus shall it thrive." As you tie the sixth say, "By the knot of six, the spell we fix." As you tie the seventh say, "By the knot of seven, the stars of heaven." As you tie the eighth say, "By the knot of eight, the hand of fate." As you tie the ninth say, "By the knot of nine, the thing is mine!"

Lay the knotted rattail cord in the center of the circle between the two candles and sit for a while seeing all of this as if it has already come true.

When you feel complete, snuff out the candles and leave every-thing right where it is. Every day, re-light the candles, sit for a while, and recite the above incantation. Save the check, the green ribbon, and the piece of cord and bury the remains of the candles along with the salt sweepings in the East.

On the day that you walk into work and ask for your raise, tie the cord around your left thigh and carry the check and the ribbon in your wallet. Everything should work out just as you wish. After you get your raise, bury the cord, the ribbon, and the check where you buried the candles and while you're at it, thank the Great Mother for her help.

CHAPTER 10

Court Spells:
Traffic, Divorce, Annoying Litigations

Going to court is one of those experiences most of us would rather avoid, but sometimes we can't. If you do end up in court for whatever reason, it's important to remember that much of what happens when you stand in front of a judge is karmic in nature and half of winning your case involves letting go of being too invested in the outcome. When the stakes are high, this is easier said than done, but we're all hip enough to know that even when things don't appear to be fair, everything is in divine order. That's why using spells in court can be tricky.

Look long and hard at the cause you are fighting for before using any of the spells that follow. Many of us righteously believe that we are right, when in fact we are in denial about things that we just refuse to confront. The seeds of our circumstances get sown in deeds that were often done long before whatever got us to the courthouse. If you are involved in a situation that appears to be unfair, look at every aspect of your past to see which choices led you to it and, for God's sake, have enough self awareness to leave well enough alone if need be, once you connect with what the real issue stems from. No spell will guarantee you a win if you are being dishonest with yourself.

On the other hand, when you are coming from a place of integrity, a good court spell will work wonders. After all, we *do* have the power to impact everything in our reality, including an uptight judge, with the clear direction of pure thought. As far as timing these spells goes, my feeling is that it really helps to have the "right" influences, but life doesn't happen in a straight line, so do the best you can and work with what you've got.

The following spell is useful in *any* legal situation. I would use this one as a matter of course whether you're dealing with a speeding ticket, a messy divorce, or a twisted-up inheritance issue.

The "Kiss Up To the Judge" Spell

WHAT YOU'LL NEED

A bay leaf candle or a purple candle
Musk incense
Musk oil
2 bay leaves
3 to 7 marigold blossoms
(use juniper berries if marigolds aren't in bloom)
A gold charm bag
A piece of parchment or paper cut from a brown paper bag
A pen
Matches
A nail

Choose *any* day to do this spell because legal trials and tribulations aren't as tuned to the natural rhythms of the Great Mother as they should be! If you *do* have a choice about which day to work on, any time during the New to Full Moon works best for attracting positive energy. Thursdays, Fridays, and Sundays are optimal for court spells. If there are a lot of papers to be signed or you want communication to be clear, choose a Wednesday.

℮ ℮ ℮

Depending on the gravity of the situation, you might want to cast a circle. Gather all of your ingredients and once the circle is cast, light your incense. With the nail, inscribe your candle with the Rune Teiwaz ↑. Anoint the candle wick to base with musk oil, set it in front of you, and light it. As the candle burns, charge the two bay leaves, the marigold blossoms or the juniper berries, and the gold charm bag one at a time in your left hand. This means holding each of them in your hand and sending your thoughts of success into each item. You don't have to spend all day at this, but you *do* need to be focused. When everything is charged, lay it all in front of the candle.

Now write on the parchment exactly what it is that you want the outcome of the case to be. Anoint the paper with seven drops of musk oil, kiss it once, and lay it in front of the candle. Take the two bay leaves and write the name of the judge or the name of the person you most want to impress on each one. As you sit with all of this energy collected in front of you, say these words out loud three times:

> My cause is just and I am free
> From any guile or hypocrisy.
> The judge will know when he sees my face
> That the forces opposing me are in disgrace.
> Grant me all of my desires
> And let my enemies be exposed as liars.

When you have finished, wrap the marigolds or the juniper berries in the piece of parchment and put them into the gold bag. If you're heading to court the next day, let the candle burn down to nothing and leave the charm bag next to it. If you have a little time before you go before the judge, snuff the candle out and re-light it for a little while each day, repeating the above incantation three times every time you do this.

On the day you go to court, place a bay leaf in each shoe. Bury the remains of the candle in the North and put the gold charm bag in your left pocket or carry it in your purse. When your court session is over, bury the charm bag and the bay leaves where you buried the candle.

Repeat this spell from start to finish if you have to make another appearance, and for every consecutive appearance. You should be quite pleased with the results.

SPELLS TO HELP YOU RESOLVE A MESSY INHERITANCE CASE

It's funny what happens when people die. We all think we know our relatives until it's time to decide who gets what. Why love, money, and death are so heavily enmeshed beats me, but they sure are. It's rare that an inheritance case goes smoothly. If the vibes are openly hostile, it's almost easier because at least you know what you're up against. It's more common that all parties are covert about their intentions, smiling to your face and plotting behind your back. What follows are a few spells that will help you make sure that everything gets evenly divided whenever things are less than fair.

The "What's Mine is Mine, Let's Be Decent About This, It's Only Fair" Spell

WHAT YOU'LL NEED

A purple candle to represent you
A white candle to represent the deceased
A blue candle for each other interested party
All of the documents relating to the situation
A piece of parchment or brown paper
with a list of what's being passed on
(If there's real estate involved, a map or
photograph of the property will help)
A piece of parchment or paper cut from a brown paper bag
A pen
A lodestone or a refrigerator magnet

Musk oil
Musk incense
A tablespoon of cinnamon powder
Scissors
2 pieces of grapevine or 2 two-foot pieces of twine
A piece of tinfoil
A nail

---·--·--·--·--·--·--·--·--·--·---

The power of a Full Moon will enhance this type of spell and will shower your magic with a thousand mega watts of good, positive energy.

ℯ ℯ ℯ

Gather all your ingredients and cast a circle. Once the circle is cast, light the incense. Inscribe the purple candle with the rune Teiwaz ↑ and the rune Othala ⋈ .

On the white candle, inscribe with the nail the name of the deceased and an equal sign (=). On each of the blue candles, inscribe the names of the parties involved and an equal sign (=). Anoint your purple candle wick to base with the musk oil. Roll it in the cinnamon powder and rub the spice into the etched symbols. Anoint the white candle and all the other candles base to wick with the same oil.

When the candles are dressed, set them up in front of you and light them. Put the white candle in the center and place the purple candle directly in front of it. Arrange the blue candles as if they are subsidiary entities, off to the side or behind the other two candles.

If you have legal documents or papers associated with the case to play with, anoint them with musk oil and place them in front of your candle along with any maps or pertinent photographs. Place the list of items being divided up under the white candle.

Now write on the piece of parchment whatever it is that you feel is your fair share, and anything else you might want to say relative to the situation. For example, if your brother is being really greedy, ask that his heart be opened to the spirit of generosity. Place this list under the purple candle and put the lodestone or the kitchen magnet on top of it. Now quietly repeat the following words out loud:

> In the name of Jupiter and all that's fair
> I ask that everyone get their share.

Now cut the list that's under the white candle along with the maps and any photographs into equal pieces so that each party or "candle" gets an equal portion of whatever it is that your cutting up. Put these pieces of paper under each candle. Don't worry about the white candle. After all, the deceased one is in the great beyond and totally free of all attachments!

With everything symbolically cut fair and square, draw the lodestone or magnet over the words you've written on the piece of parchment that you placed under your candle as you say the following words out loud seven times:

> *The all-seeing eye of truth and love*
> *Shines down and sees from far above*
> *That everything that I've asked for is rightly mine,*
> *And with that fact all parties are fine.*

Now draw the blue candles and every scrap of paper under them together in a bundle with the white center candle. Wrap them once around with the grapevine or twine. Bring your candle to the bundle and wrap the grapevine or twine around everything one or two times more. Keep the list you've made of what you want with the magnet on top of it next to everything and let all of the candles burn down to nothing.

If you can't do this in one sitting, snuff everything out and take a little time each day to re-light every candle and repeat the incantation above seven times. When all the candles have burned down to nothing and all the scraps of paper have been covered with melted wax, wrap what's left in the tinfoil. Wrap the paper with your list and the magnet around the ball of foil with the second piece of vine or twine.

Keep this charm under your pillow or under your bed along with the pertinent legal documents until the day the case goes to court. On that day, put all the documents wherever they need to be, bury the charm in the West, and watch and see where the chips fall.

The following is another spell that you can use when there's an inheritance at stake. It's less of a "production" than the last one but just as effective.

The "Wheel of Fortune" Spell

WHAT YOU'LL NEED

A white candle
As many green candles as there are relatives,
litigants, whatever
As many 1-foot pieces of purple satin ribbon
as there are relatives, litigants, whatever
As many coins as there are relatives, litigants, whatever
As many lodestones or kitchen magnets as there
are relatives, litigants, whatever
Musk oil
Musk incense
3 tablespoons of cinnamon powder
A red satin or velvet pouch
A nail

Use a New to Full Moon for this one and any Thursday, Friday, or Sunday will do.

℮ ℮ ℮

Gather all of your ingredients and cast a circle. With the nail, inscribe the white candle with the name of the person the inheritance is coming from. Inscribe the green candles with your name and the name of each relative along with an equal sign (=). Anoint the white candle base to wick with the musk oil. Anoint the green candles wick to base with the musk oil and roll them in the cinnamon powder.

Light the white candle, set it up in the center, and surround it with the green candles. Light all of the green candles in a clockwise direction starting with your candle first. Lay the purple satin ribbons down so that they extend from the white center candle to each of the green candles, like the spokes of a wheel. Place the coins around the center candle and place the lodestones or the magnets at the base of each green candle on top of the purple ribbon. Put three drops of musk oil along the length of each ribbon and say these words out loud three times:

> *The wheel of life has brought us here,*
> *It's time to receive what we hold dear.*
> *The force that draws it is more than fair,*
> *Every one will get an equal share.*

As you say this, slide the coins from the center candle along the length of each ribbon to each of the green candles. Sit for a moment and let the magnetic energy build. Now snuff out all of the candles and leave the "wheel of fortune" where it is.

Every night thereafter, light the candles for a little while and repeat the above incantation three times. Do this until all the candles have burned down. Bury the white candle in the North. Wrap each ribbon, coin, and magnet up with whatever's left of each candle and place it all inside the red charm bag.

Carry this bag with you, hang it from your bedpost, or sleep with it under your pillow until everything is resolved. On the day that the final decision is made, carry this charm in your pocket or purse. When everything is fully resolved, bury the pouch in the West or throw it into the nearest body of moving water.

AND NOW IT'S TIME TO GET DIVORCED

If you've made it to menopause without getting divorced, all I can say is "wow." Most of us have been through this at least once. For those of you who haven't, you don't know what you're missing!

For some strange reason, even though women get the short end of the stick in other areas, we actually have the upper hand in divorce cases if we know enough to take it. The kicker here is that by the time you're a crone, you're usually worth a lot more than you were when you tied the knot. This may not be true in every case. Many of us brought more to the relationship right from the start. This creates problems if your partner is the type who's wily enough to twist up the equal rights thing and use that to get you to bend over and give up the family jewels. If you're getting divorced and there's a risk that your old man/lady might press for more than his/her fair share of the assets, use the following spell.

The "Hey, Hold on There, Buster, This Stuff Is Mine!" Spell

WHAT YOU'LL NEED

A red candle to represent you
A blue candle to represent your spouse
Photographs of the jointly held or individually owned assets
(If you don't have these then draw up
a list with everything on it)
Maps of any jointly or individually held real estate
(If you don't have these then draw them yourself)
A piece of parchment or paper cut from a brown paper bag
A pen
A lodestone or a refrigerator magnet
A piece of tinfoil

2 feet of twine
3 tablespoons of sea salt
3 tablespoons of cinnamon powder
Musk oil
Patchouli oil
Musk incense
A red satin or velvet charm bag
A nail

--.--.--.--.--.--.--.--.--.--

Start this spell at the New Moon and let the energy it creates build till the Moon gets full.

ℯ ℯ ℯ

Gather all of your ingredients and cast a circle. With the nail, inscribe your name and the Othala rune ᛟ along with the Fehu rune ᚠ into your candle. Anoint your candle wick to base with musk oil and roll it in the cinnamon powder. Carve your partner's name along with the Isa rune | into the blue candle. Anoint your partner's candle base to wick with patchouli oil.

Now set up the red candle in front of you, light it, and place all relevant maps, photographs, legal documents, or lists underneath it. Place the lodestone or kitchen magnet on top of all these papers. Set the blue candle behind the red candle about a foot away and spark it up.

Cast a circle of sea salt around the red candle and the papers. When this is done and all your interests are protected, say the following words out loud seven times:

What's mine is mine
And can never belong
To anyone else but me.
My spouse is frozen and powerless to take

Any of what lies here.
This circle of salt protects me,
And I have nothing to fear.

Snuff out the blue candle, wrap it tightly in the tinfoil, and tie it with twine. Set this charm behind you and sit for a while with the red candle as you visualize what you want to happen.

When you are totally clear, write down in your own words exactly what you want the result of all of this to be. Anoint the paper with three drops of musk oil, kiss it once, and place it inside the circle underneath the lodestone or magnet.

When you feel complete, snuff out the red candle and leave everything where it is. Bury the charm of tinfoil and twine in the North at least three miles away. As you do this, point with your right hand to the spot where you buried it and say:

In no way will this spell reverse or cast upon me any curse.

Every day, until the Moon is full, re-light the red candle, activate the circle, and meditate on your intentions. On the night of the Full Moon, wrap the remains of the candle in all of the papers, sweep the salt into this bundle along with the magnet or the lodestone, and place it in the red charm bag. Tie the charm bag to your bed-post, sleep with it under your pillow, or carry it in your purse until the case is resolved. When everything's said and done, burn the bag and scatter the ashes in the nearest body of moving water.

SPELL TO MAKE THAT
SPEEDING TICKET NULL AND VOID

Speeding tickets are an expensive nuisance. If you weren't able to sway the cop who stopped you with your charm or a sweet and submissive attitude, use this spell on the day you have to show up in traffic court to contest the ticket.

The "Life in the Fast Lane" Spell

WHAT YOU'LL NEED

A white candle
2 tablespoons of coffee
Musk oil
Musk incense
A bottle of white correction fluid
2 bay leaves
Your copy of the ticket
A photocopy of your ticket
A nail

Needless to say, you can't pick your day in court. If it happens to fall on a Wednesday, however, all the better, because Wednesday rules cars, traffic, communication, and the mundane hassles of ordinary life.

℮ ℮ ℮

Light the incense and with the nail, inscribe the Teiwaz rune ↑ on the candle. Anoint the candle base to wick with the musk oil and roll it in the coffee. Coffee is useful whenever you want to speed up someone's mental processes, and in this type of situation, you want the judge to flash on the fact that you are in the right.

Light the candle and set it in front of you with the copies of the ticket. Now write the name of the judge on one of the bay leaves. Write the name of the police officer who stopped you on the other. Place both bay leaves on either side of the candle.

Sit for a few minutes and then say the following words out loud three times:

> I am free and the judge will see
> That none of this applies to me.

*'X' is the symbol, 'X' is the sign
That will keep me from having to pay this fine.*

Now take the correction fluid and draw a white "X" on both copies of the ticket. Let the candle burn and visualize yourself going into the court room and having everything dismissed. *Save the bay leaves and the original copy of the ticket in a safe spot!* Snuff out the candle, wrap the photocopy of the ticket around it, and bury it all in the West.

When you go to court, put a bay leaf in each shoe and keep the original copy of the ticket in your left pocket. If you have to pres-ent the ticket to the judge and he/she asks you why it looks the way it does, tell him (or her) that one of your grandchildren was being artistic! It will probably give them something to laugh about and lighten up the atmosphere favorably. Don't worry about the out-come, fate will twist and everything will turn around in your favor.

SPELL TO COUNTERACT THE NEGATIVE IMPACT OF ANY LAWSUIT FILED AGAINST YOU UNJUSTLY

Every now and then someone decides to blame you for something you didn't do. Because we live in a litigious society, petty disputes can land us in court. When you're being legally hassled by someone, the best thing to do is "Bottle" them (see p. 76). Or you can simply use the following spell to make this type of problem evaporate.

The "God, You're Such a Nuisance, Please Disappear" Spell

WHAT YOU'LL NEED

A red candle to represent you
A black votive candle to represent the thorn in your side
Patchouli incense

Patchouli oil
Musk oil
4 iron nails
A lodestone or a refrigerator magnet
4 tablespoons of sea salt
A piece of parchment or paper cut from a brown paper bag
A mayonnaise jar
A sheet of tinfoil
2 to 3 feet of twine
A cup of dirt
Any papers or documents relating to the case

This spell should be started just as the Moon starts to wane so that whatever you focus your intentions on will lose its force and slowly vanish.

℮ ℮ ℮

Gather all your ingredients together. For this spell, you'll definitely need to cast a circle. Whenever you're dealing with a nutcase, it's good to insulate yourself as much as possible against his or her vibration because even unconscious, ignorant people have energy patterns that float around the astral plane. You certainly don't want all their "critters" and gremlins messing up your spell!

Once the circle is cast, light the incense. Carve your name and the Teiwaz rune ↑ into the red candle. Carve the black candle with the name of your adversary(ies) and the Isa rune |. Anoint the red candle base to wick with musk oil. Anoint the black candle wick to base with the patchouli oil. Roll the red candle in the sea salt, and reserve what's left of the salt for later. Set up the red candle in front of you and light it. Light the black candle and place it about a foot behind the red one. Anoint any of the papers or documents relating to the case with musk oil, kiss them once, and place them under the red candle.

Now take the four nails and lay them with the sharp ends pointing out around the red candle and the documents. You should place one pointing out at the North, East, South, and West, in that order. Encircle all this with the sea salt, making sure that the nails are inside the circle. When this is set up, say these words out loud seven times:

> The lies and deception directed at me
> Will have no effect because I am free
> From anything my enemies say or do
> To cut my reputation in two.
> This circle of protection forms a shield so strong,
> It's I who am right and they who are wrong.

Let the red candle burn while you write down on the parchment your intentions in this situation. Place these intentions in the center of the circle on top of all your documents and set the lodestone or magnet on top of everything.

Now it's time to bind your opponent. Wrap the black candle tightly in the sheet of tinfoil and bind it as fast as you can with the twine. Pop this charm into the mayonnaise jar and bury it with the cup of dirt. Put the lid on the jar and snuff out the red candle, leaving the circle of protection right where it is. Grab a shovel, hop in your car and take a drive toward the West (or take a long walk in that direction). Find a secluded spot where you can bury the jar. Once it's in the ground, point to it with your right hand and say:

> Evil return to source
> Impelled by incredible force.
> In the name of what's right and free,
> I am protected,
> So mote it be!

Walk away from the spot and don't look back. Re-light the red candle once a day thereafter and repeat the first incantation three times. Sit quietly in a state of focus and concentration, visualizing everything turning in your favor.

When the Moon is new again, take the remains of the candle, the four nails, and the salt sweepings and wrap them inside the piece of parchment that has your intentions written on it. Place all the legal documents wherever they need to be and bury the remains of the circle in the Eastern portion of your property. Cover the spot with a large rock to protect it, and let the powers that be serve your highest good from this point on.

CHAPTER 11

Can't Find Your Car Keys and Other Life-Is-Nuts Spells

A nd finally I'm including a bunch of whacky spells because life gets crazy when you're a crone. I think this happens because our minds are functioning at a much higher, faster frequency and our *reality* is constant; it's vibrating the way it always did. I may be fooling myself here, but it's how I've chosen to explain it to myself!

The fact that so much wisdom becomes available to us when we reach menopause is wonderful, but it comes with a few pitfalls. Take memory, for instance. As our pineal gland reawakens, some of the information stored there gets lost before it reaches our left brain. Either that or our left brain can't *process* what our Higher Self is feeding it. The side effect is that we can get really spaced out sometimes. It's easier to joke about memory loss than it is to live with what it does to you!

Some of the spells included in this chapter are designed to help bridge the gap that the circuits in our brain can't cross. Others help you maintain a sense of humor as your body and brain start to misbehave in the crone years. Now that our third eyes are wide open, we have an edge that younger women will have to wait to acquire. The goddess hype has its place and it's wonderful to rhapsodize about those mysteries, but the "Great Secret of Cronehood" is quite simple. After years of trying to be a goddess, all we find on the other side of the menopausal portal is that it's totally okay to be as nuts as you want!

SPELLS TO HELP YOU FIND YOUR GLASSES, CAR KEYS, WALLET AND ANYTHING ELSE THAT'S MISSING

When things disappear, it's my opinion that the gnomes and elemental spirits that are our "familiars" are actually *helping* us. They know that we either need to slow down or be held up in order to avoid something disastrous or unpleasant. For instance, the half hour you spend rooting through everything in your house to find your glasses is often just enough time to bypass a fender bender or the possibility of bumping into one of those "time sucking voids" you often meet at the supermarket.

The first thing you need to do when something essential like your glasses, car keys, or wallet is lost in space is relax and realize that this is a *good* thing. To *find* what you're looking for, it also helps to know how gnomes and elementals operate. They like to barter and trade, so if you make a deal with them, they will be more than happy to return your lost object. The following spell usually works. It's an "oldie" and I can't even remember where I found it. To be honest, I don't even know why it works, but I have a feeling that the reasons are buried in antiquity and don't need to be explained or questioned.

The "Come Out, Come Out, Wherever You Are" Spell

WHAT YOU'LL NEED

A red bandana
A handful of dirt
A penny

Place the handful of soil in the bandana and tie it up in a knot. Bury this charm outside somewhere or shove it into a potted plant. As you do this say these words out loud:

Back to the earth back to the ground
Wherever you are you will surely be found.
I'll trade this cloth and the soil inside
If what's been lost will cease to hide.

Relax and go about your business. Within an hour, you will find what you're looking for or someone else will. When this happens, go and dig up the red bandana, untie it, return the soil inside to the earth, saying, "Thank you" to whoever brought it back. Leave a penny in the spot where you dug up the charm.

If that spell doesn't work, here's one that works wonders and will keep you busy while you're waiting for your stuff to turn up.

The "Let's Make a Deal" Spell

What you'll need

A penny
A nail
A small rock
A bone
A red bandana or a cotton handkerchief

Obviously this can be done any time you misplace something and need to find it.

℮ ℮ ℮

Put the penny, nail, rock, and bone in the center of the handkerchief and tie this into a bundle. Then say these words out loud:

I'll give you a penny, I'll give you a nail,
I'll give you a rock and a bone.

If you return my (glasses, car keys, wallet, money,
   diamond ring) to me,
All this will be your own.

Take this little satchel and bury it in the ground outside your door. You can also hide it somewhere in your house or office, if that seems more appropriate. Go about your business and stop dwelling on finding what you're looking for. Take a walk, take a bath, eat a piece of cake, or do some housework. Within an hour, you'll find what you're looking for or someone else will.

If you *don't* find it, then whatever you're offering in trade isn't worth enough to the gnomes. You'll have to up the ante! In that case, dig up the handkerchief and replace the penny, nail, rock, and bone with something more valuable. Go to your jewelry box, your button jar, or your junk drawer and find four shiny objects or anything that you think a gnome would find more pleasing, place them inside the hanky, and re-bury it or hide it in the same spot.

If you have to repeat this procedure, then you will need to use a different incantation. For these more "materialistic" elemental spirits, try saying the following words out loud:

I'll give you a ring, I'll give you a charm,
I'll give you a button, and a ribbon.
If you return my (glasses, car keys, wallet, money,
   diamond ring) to me,
All will be forgiven.

Here is another " lost object" spell for those of you who don't have the time to mess around with elementals and gnomes!

The "Odin's Eye" Spell

WHAT YOU'LL NEED

A piece of paper

A pen or marker
Scissors

You can light a candle if you want to, but consider this the express route to finding lost items. You don't have to make a big deal out of it.

Draw a picture of an eye on the piece of paper and cut it out. Leave enough room on the paper to draw the Pertho rune ⟨ and cut it out in the shape of a circle smaller then the eye. Hold the eye up to your third eye and focus your mind on the missing item for a few minutes. Lay the eye down in front of you and hold the Pertho rune up to your third eye, still focusing on whatever you've lost or misplaced. When you're all clear, lay the rune on top of the eye and say the following words out loud three times:

> *The all-seeing eye inside my head*
> *knows exactly where everything lies.*
> *It looks into the Well of Mimir and*
> *knows every secret surprise.*
> *As soon as I stop moaning what's*
> *lost it will magically reappear,*
> *The all-seeing eye inside my head*
> *will make everything perfectly clear.*

Hang out, fix yourself a cup of coffee, and wait. You should have the lost object in your hands within the hour.

SPELL TO USE WHEN MERCURY'S RETROGRADE

When Mercury turns retrograde–about three times a year–Murphy's Law is at the wheel! Cars break down. Computers do things that are inconvenient and costly. Letters get lost in the mail and every type of communication gets tangled. People change their minds about things they were clear as a bell about before. Misunderstandings are par for the course because there's a tendency to not even hear what's being said. Legal issues get postponed and court dates get changed or key people just don't show up. This retrograde state lasts about three weeks.

Because we've been raised to believe that life goes in a straight line, the detours we take when Mercury is retrograde confuse, annoy, and upset us. The simplest way to deal with Mercury when it's retrograde is just to *know* that nothing that gets decided, stated, or acted upon now will be the last word. Whatever you do, don't sign contracts, buy cars or appliances, or decide to break up (or make up) with your lover when this influence is in effect. It's good to know when this influence is operative because it makes it easier to have a sense of humor about the crazy things it does.

From a cosmic perspective, this phenomenon functions as a regulating influence. It adjusts things and gives us all time to rethink our plans just enough to make everything happen exactly when it needs to and not a moment sooner. It helps us to make sure we know what we want and actually disengages the gears of the universe long enough for the rest of the planets to align themselves, fall into the proper slot, and continue spinning.

Use your astrological calendar to mark off these three-week periods. It will save you so many headaches. The following charm is more or less like a flu shot. Use it to make yourself immune to the side effects of retrograde Mercury.

The "Magical, Mercurial Mystery Tour" Spell

WHAT YOU'LL NEED

A silver candle to represent Mercury
A photograph of yourself
6 tablespoons of sea salt
A marble
A quart-sized Mason jar
3 drops of musk oil
Nuts, bolts, and screws from the junk drawer
3 stamps, 3 envelopes, a piece of paper, and a pen

Old fuses, batteries, paper clips, tacks, and wires
A pair of wax lips or a picture of a mouth
Water
A flat stone

You have no choice about when to do this. You have to do it the day before Mercury goes retrograde, or on the day you find out it already *is* retrograde.

℮ ℮ ℮

Carve the symbol for the planet Mercury into the silver candle and anoint it wick to base with musk oil. (You'll find all the planetary symbols in Important Stuff to Know, II.) Set it in front of you on top of your photograph. Cast a circle of salt around the candle and the photo, starting at the North and moving clockwise. This arrangement represents the fact that you and your relationship to Mercury are undisturbed and safe. Now draw the marble over the candle flame three times and charge it to be a "surrogate" Mercury for the next three weeks. Let the marble be the one to take on all the retrograde effects. As you do this, say these words out loud:

> On this day and in this hour,
> I charge you to absorb all of Mercury's power
> That isn't doing me any good,
> So that life will function as it should.

Place the marble into the Mason jar along with all the nuts, bolts, stamps, envelopes, paper, pen, batteries, fuses, wires, paper clips, and tacks, as well as the mouth. Draw the Isa rune | onto a flat stone and place it on top of all the junk in the jar. Cover everything with water and put the lid on the jar. Now say the following words out loud three times:

The trouble that comes when Mercury's backwards
  won't trouble me one bit.
I have a surrogate planet taking charge of these problems
  now that the real one has quit.
All of my plans and mechanical issues will work out
  totally fine,
Everything runs like clockwork in this little world of mine.

Now put the jar in the freezer. Leave it there until Mercury goes direct. Snuff out the silver candle and leave it where it is. Re-light it for a little while every day until Mercury turns around. On that day, bury the remains of the candle along with the jar in the North corner of your property.

CAR SPELLS AND CHARMS

The main reason for car spells is for safety on the road. We head down the highway every day without knowing what will happen. Sometimes an astrological aspect that we're totally unaware of is making us more accident-prone. I use car spells as an extra form of insurance that pumps up my immunity to bad aspects, drunk drivers, fender benders, and whatever crawls out from behind my blind spot. Where I live you don't even need to lock your car, but if you live in the city, there's always car theft to consider. There are a million and one car spells, but here are a few that I use on a regular basis.

Protect Your Car and Everyone In It

Clean a quartz crystal in sea salt and water for twenty-four hours and charge it mentally with the intention for safety on the road. Include thoughts to the effect that there will be no accidents or mechanical difficulties of any kind and make the car immune to state cops, speed traps, and traffic tickets. Keep in mind that a crystal can hold as many "programs" as it has facets, so don't load it up with too much information.

Store the crystal in a silver pouch and hang it from your rearview mirror or keep it in your glove compartment. Clean and recharge the crystal once a month at the Full Moon.

The "On the Road" Spell

Here's another car spell that requires no paraphernalia. Before you leave on a trip, walk clockwise around your car three times and say the following words each time you get to the front of the car:

> *I travel here, I travel there, I go both near and far,*
> *Wherever I am on the road of life Great Spirit*
> *protects this car.*

After the last repetition, trace the Eihwaz ᛇ and the Raido ᚱ runes with your right forefinger on the hood of the car.

The "Safe Travels" Charm

WHAT YOU'LL NEED

A tablespoon each of lavender, rosemary, and mint
A "wheat" penny
A white cotton handkerchief
A yellow satin ribbon

Here's a simple charm you can make to keep yourself safe while traveling. Tie the lavender, rosemary, mint, and the penny in the white cotton handkerchief with a yellow satin ribbon. Charge the charm in your left hand with thoughts of safety on the road. Hang this magical sachet from your rearview mirror or store it anywhere in your car. Once a month when the Moon is new, wash the hanky and replace all the ingredients with fresh ones, recharging the charm with your thoughts each time you renew its contents.

Running out of gas is always a bummer! Because forgetfulness is part of life on "planet crone," it's not uncommon for us to be driving along and notice that we're almost out of gas. Your belief in mind over matter comes in handy at times like this, but it doesn't hurt to have a little backup. There are a million psychic tricks you can use for the out-of-gas thing, but the following charm is a no-brainer. It's something that you should keep in your car all the time the same as you would jumper cables or windshield washer fluid. Since you never know when you're going to run out of fuel, you can make this charm anytime just to have it ready.

The "Running on Empty" Charm

WHAT YOU'LL NEED

A piece of coal
3 small flat stones
A marker
A picture of a camel
A red velvet pouch

Draw the Raido ᚱ Eihwaz ᛇ, and Pertho ᛈ runes on the stones. Hold them in your left hand with the piece of coal and focus on the idea of the endless reserves of fuel in your gas tank. Wrap the stones inside the picture of the camel, place everything in the red pouch, and say these words aloud three times:

My car knows how to make itself go,
There are reserves on which it can pull.
It matters not what the meter reads,
My gas tank is always full.

Write down these words on a piece of paper and slip it into the pouch. When you're running on empty, take the charm bag out of the glove compartment and recite the above spell out loud till you get to the gas station. The energy from the coal, the image of the camel, and the power of the runes in this charm will take the edge off your tension whenever you find yourself low on gas. Replace and renew the charm after each use.

CHARMS FOR AIR AND WATER TRAVEL
(YES, ERICA JONG, YOUR HEART WILL GO ON AND ON!)

I don't think any charm can take away your fear of flying, but if you're superstitious or paranoid about air travel, what follows is a recipe for a little "mojo" bag that you can take with you whenever you have to get on a plane and go somewhere.

The "Archangel Michael Flies With Me" Charm

WHAT YOU'LL NEED

A sky-blue charm bag
A small vial of witchhazel
3 poplar leaves
A tablespoon each of mustard seeds,
alfalfa seeds, and celery seeds
3 feathers
Some kelp (use kelp if you'll be flying over any body of water)
A sky-blue candle (optional)

If you want to light a candle while you make this bag, go ahead. It's OK to give this a ceremonial touch, but it's not necessary. Charge all of the ingredients one at a time in your left hand with thoughts of landing safely. Fill the bag with each item, and as you do this, call on the presence of the Archangel Michael to fly along with you. Keep the charm bag close by your side during your trip. Let it serve to remind you that you are safe and in good hands.

Whenever you travel by water, don't let your "Titanic" pictures get the best of you! Whether you're just out for a day sail or taking a ride on the Queen Mary, the following charm will allay your fears of going down with the ship.

The "Unsinkable Molly Brown" Charm

WHAT YOU'LL NEED

A blue-green satin charm bag
2 corks
Some kelp
3 tablespoons of sea salt
3 shallots
A sea-green candle

Light the candle as you make this charm. Fire antidotes the energy of water. Charge all of the ingredients in your left hand with thoughts of a safe arrival and place them in the bag, one at a time. Call on the power of the planet Neptune to protect you while you're at sea and say these words out loud:

> *Whenever I am on the sea,*
> *King Neptune watches over me.*

Take the charm bag with you on the boat. Your fears will sink and you will float!

UNSOLVED MYSTERIES

We all get into situations where things are hard to read. Not everyone has the time to become a soothsayer, but there is a way to divine the truth about what's going on without being a full-blown psychic. When you want to get to the bottom of something, use the following trick.

The "Which End Is Up?" Magical Oracle

WHAT YOU'LL NEED

As many flat stones as you have possibilities
(Technically you should use chicken bones for this, but it takes so
much time. If you're a purist, go for it.
Cook up a chicken until the meat falls off
and leave the bones to dry in the sun until they turn white.)
A box with a hole cut in the lid
big enough for your hand to fit through
A black marker

On each stone or bone write down a symbol or a word that defines a particular option, possibility, or outcome. Pop the stones or bones into the box and as you shake it, say the following words out loud:

> *Behind all this confusion,*
> *One thing is clear and true.*
> *What's false deceives and is illusion,*
> *What's real will come right through.*

Reach into the box and pull out one of the bones or stones. Whichever one you draw will hold the truth in the situation. Place your "answer" on a sunny window ledge so that the solar light will act to bring everything out into the open.

UNWANTED VISITORS

We've all been cursed with people who show up uninvited. Sometimes they stay for weeks and sometimes you can't get rid of them at all! We were all raised to be so damned polite, but in situations like this, it doesn't work in our favor. It mystifies me why, when the person who's parked themselves in your space indefinitely is being so visible about their rudeness, we feel uncomfortable or unkind being rude right back.

If you know in advance that someone you dislike intensely is about to descend on you and drive you crazy, try the following spell. If it happens that they decide to just show up, you can use it after their arrival and it will work just as well. Usually what happens is they get called away by some twist of fate and will head off merrily to annoy someone else.

The "Don't Come Around Here No More" Spell

WHAT YOU'LL NEED

A photograph of your house
An 8 1/2 x 11 piece of paper
Glue
A pen
A black candle
Patchouli oil
Patchouli incense
A nail

A waning Moon is best for this but since you never know when uninvited guests will arrive you can do this spell anytime.

℮ ℮ ℮

Gather all your ingredients and cast a circle. Light your incense and with the nail, inscribe the Thurisaz rune ᚦ, the Isa rune ᛁ, and the name of your unwanted visitor into the candle. Anoint the candle base to wick with patchouli oil, light it, and set it in front of you. Glue the photo of your house onto the paper and draw a circular border of Thurisaz runes around the picture, making sure that the point of the rune faces out.

Now write the name of the unwanted guest on the paper outside of the circle of runes. After you've done this, say the following words out loud seven times:

> You never call or take time to request
> Whether you're welcome here.
> If I ever wanted you to be my guest,
> I would have already made that clear.
> Since it's impolite to be rude and never OK to shout,
> These runes will say what needs to be said,
> Just don't let the door hit you on the way out!"

Place the paper charm underneath your front doormat and let the candle burn all the way down to nothing. Your "long lost friend" will either change his mind and not come at all or he will suddenly be called away on a mission or emergency that causes him to have to say goodbye. After he leaves or by the next New Moon, bury the candle along with the paper charm in the North corner of your property.

Making Migraines Fun

You're going to like this one! I've never had a migraine, but it seems as if crones are more susceptible to them than are younger women. Some people say that they come with menopause. Since I'm no expert on the subject, I've had to check other sources. Louise Hay says in her book *Heal Your Body* that the underlying emotional cause of a migraine is anger at being driven too hard by yourself or someone else. According to her, they also have something to do with one's reluctance to go with the flow of life. Perhaps the first thing every migraine sufferer needs to do is lighten up, but if you're a long-term control freak, that might take time and a little therapy. So what do you do in the meantime? Ms. Hay says that to get rid of a migraine, the best thing to do is masturbate!

In thinking about this, my first thought was, "Would you be motivated to masturbate if you were in that much pain?" I've interviewed several of my friends who have tried this "spell" and they say it really works, so the *moment* you feel the headache coming on, which is apparently something that a lot of migraine sufferers recognize, whip off your clothes, plug in the vibrator, and go for it! Don't bother to cast a circle, light a candle, or burn incense for this one. I have a feeling you won't have time!

INSOMNIA

Another delightful little blessing of cronehood is insomnia. With each passing year, we become more and more familiar with the middle of the night. Lying awake all night is such an interesting process. I don't have a TV, and for some reason reading isn't something that interests me in the middle of the night. I can't get any work done, and housework, which would be great to get out of the way in the wee hours of the morning, is the last thing I think of doing. When insomnia strikes, it feels as if my mind has some heretofore unexplored territory it wants me to discover and I spend hours trying to figure out how to get there. The saying, "Tomorrow never comes" is a total lie when you're a menopausal insomniac. It hits you like a ton of bricks!

Toe Tapping Your Way to Sleep

Instead of giving you a spell for insomnia, I'm going to go all out here and offer you a very simple cure! When you wake up at night knowing inside that you'll never get back to sleep, roll down the covers and sit up in bed with your legs together straight out in front of you. Lean back on your arms a little with your elbows straight the way you do sometimes when you're sitting at the beach. With your feet pointing up to the ceiling, waggle them back and forth at least 150 times like a pair of windshield wipers, tapping your toes together in the middle. This is called "toe tapping" and it releases all the blocked "Chi" energy that's keeping you awake. I guarantee this.

It works every time. You can light a candle if you want to, but make sure you blow it out before you fall asleep!

DEALING WITH DEPRESSION, BAD MOODS, BITCHINESS, & HORMONAL INSANITY

You know I never had much of this. There was a year or so where the people I'm close to told me I was unbearable, but in retrospect all that was happening was that I was starting to speak up for the first time and it wasn't okay with them. Well, maybe I was a little psychotic, but now I realize that it's totally normal to be nuts sometimes. I've heard some of my fellow crones complain about mood swings. Most of them are on hormones so go figure? I am proud to say that I did menopause "cold turkey," and in the long run I think it's easier and better for you. I'm very opinionated about this, but don't worry. I'm not here to preach. A "girl's gotta do what a girl's gotta do," and if you have to take hormones, I won't argue with you. The point here is that we all get depressed or crazy for periods of time until "The Change" is complete. When you notice that you're ready to call the men in the white suits, or spiraling down into the "well of weird," try the following spell.

The "Ready for the Nut House" Spell

WHAT YOU'LL NEED

A white candle
Lavender oil
Frankincense incense
A nail
A lodestone or refrigerator magnet
4 tablespoons of sea salt
2 bowls filled with fresh spring water
A pot of chamomile tea and a cup

Don't worry about casting a circle or what the Moon is doing. When you're feeling this crazy, none of these things matter. Light the incense and let it purify the space. With the nail, inscribe your name into the white candle, as well as the words, "I am one with all life." Anoint it wick to base with the lavender oil and set it to burn in front of you. Place a bowl on either side of the candle and cast a circle of salt around everything, starting at the North and moving in a clockwise motion. Pick up the bowl of water on the left and hold it to your lips. Breathe all of your sadness into it or say all the words that you can't say and let the water receive that energy. Place the magnet into the water and set the bowl down on the floor behind you. Now pick up the bowl of water on the right and hold it up to your lips. Breathe all of what you wish and long for with words or sighs into the water and set it inside the circle next to the candle again. Bring the bowl of water that you placed behind you outside and pour it into the ground, burying the magnet in the same spot. Go back inside, sit down in front of the candle, and say the following words out loud, one, three, or seven times, whatever feels best to you:

> Sorrow and joy are one and the same,
> But today it's hard to see
> Who I am in the scheme of things and why I came to be.
> I give all my sadness to Mother Earth and know that
>   she's here to hold me,
> The water here will remove every fear,
> And release me enough to feel free and clear.

Pour a cup of chamomile tea and add it to the water in the bowl. Drink all of the water out of the bowl, and as it goes down see yourself being filled with the joyous energy you breathed into it. Go take a bath or a shower, snuff out the candle, and if you can, crawl into bed and take a nap. When you wake up, re-light the candle and reflect on the words you carved into it. Sit for a while in the candlelight and meditate, pray, or dance. You will feel better within two hours, if you don't already.

WITCH'S BREW

I used to work in a wharf bar in Gloucester, Massachusetts. Bartending is a lot like witchcraft. I spent a lot of time "inventing" drinks and realized one day that a cocktail is basically a potion. Here is my all time favorite "potion." Unless you've got alcohol issues, I recommend using this any time you need an elixir instead of a spell.

"Mother of the Skye's Magnificent Margarita"

WHAT YOU'LL NEED:

A shaker glass filled with ice
A saucer with 3 tablespoons of kosher salt
2 shots of good tequila
A healthy shot of Cointreau
The juice from 3 limes
A squirt of soda water
A margarita glass–and some ice to fill it
if you want it on the rocks

Rub the rim of the glass with the fruit side of the lime rind. Press the rim into the saucer of salt and set the glass on the counter. Pour two shots of tequila into the shaker glass. Add the Cointreau, the lime juice, and the soda water. Shake this well and strain it into the margarita glass. Put your feet up and reflect on the beauty of life. Isn't it wonderful that in a politically correct world, a crone can do anything she damn well pleases! Raise a glass to yourself, laugh, and remember how wonderful you are.

Important Stuff to Know, I
Runic Symbols and Their Meanings

Fehu	ᚠ	Fehu rules abundance and one's ability to create and maintain it.
Uruz	ᚢ	Uruz is a symbol of strength and endurance. It also rules health.
Thurisaz	ᚦ	Thurisaz is used to bind, fetter, or control any force that appears stronger than you are. It is a protective rune.
Ansuz	ᚨ	Ansuz rules communication and messages. Ansuz releases fetters. It also rules the wind.
Raido	ᚱ	Raido rules every type of journey. It also rules choices and knowledge of right and wrong.
Kenaz	ᚲ	Kenaz rules intuitive knowing and the light within. It symbolizes the power of positive thinking.
Gebo	ᚷ	Gebo rules relationships of any kind. It rules legally binding contracts and gifts.
Wunjo	ᚹ	Wunjo rules joy and happiness.
Hagalaz	ᚺ	Rules the past and its ability to influence the present. It rules frost and hail. Hagalaz is disruptive and it functions to install change.
Nauthiz	ᚾ	Nauthiz rules need, fear, guilt, and the need for patience
Isa	ᛁ	Isa rules ice. It freezes things and keeps everything exactly the way it is. It has the power to halt things indefinitely.

Jera	ᛡ	Jera rules yule, the Sun, change, and the concept of cycles that repeat and return.
Eihwaz	ᛃ	Eihwaz protects things. It is connected to the Tree of Life and has tremendous power.
Pertho	ᛈ	Pertho has to do with the secrets of the unseen world and whatever is hidden.
Algiz	ᛉ	Algiz shields, protects, and defends.
Sowelo	ᛋ	Sowelo rules the intervention of your Higher Self and the positive impact this creates. It has to do with the impact of karma.
Teiwaz	↑	Teiwaz is a victory rune. It is strong, positive, and cannot fail.
Berkana	ᛒ	Berkana rules birth and children. It also has to do with the gestation phase of any process.
Ehwaz	M	Ehwaz rules horses and our ability to adjust, cooperate and form partnerships. Marriage is ruled by this rune.
Mannaz	ᛘ	Mannaz rules the collective, or mankind as a whole. It speaks to the double joy we create the moment we realize we are all one. Groups are ruled by this rune, as is the common good.
Laguz	ᚱ	Laguz rules the power of Water. It is feminine, psychic, and receptive. It shows whether or not our plans are riding on a favorable tide. Laguz is also a love rune.
Inguz	◊	Inguz rules what we inherit from our ancestors along with change and evolution. It rules DNA, completion, growth, and fulfillment.
Othila or *Othala*	ᛟ	Othala has to do with property and ownership. What we own is often what we inherit. It symbolizes security and safety also.
Dagaz	ᛞ	Dagaz rules day. It relates to changes that evolve and to the infinite cycles that life revolves in. It is outside of time and space and therefore magic. Dagaz can be used to make things invisible.

Important Stuff to Know, II
Planetary Symbols and What They Rule

☉ *The Sun* / Rules Sunday, success, happiness, fulfillment, light, heat, and joy.

☽ *The Moon* / Rules Monday, female energy, emotions, children, and the home.

♂ *Mars* / Rules Tuesday, male energy, sex, initiative, triumph, confidence, and victory.

☿ *Mercury* / Rules Wednesday, paper, writing, communication, travel, siblings, and speed.

♃ *Jupiter* / Rules Thursday, expansion, luck, faith, prosperity, generosity, and good will.

♀ *Venus* / Rules Friday, love, money, romance, beauty, and the arts.

♄ *Saturn* / Rules Saturday, coldness, darkness, winter, death, age, restrictions, and blight.

♅ *Uranus* / Rules electricity, invention, eccentricity, the future, astrology, the occult, the unexpected, and groups.

♆ *Neptune* / Rules fantasy, illusions, deception, spirituality, psychics, acting, water, fog, and disillusionment.

♇ *Pluto* / Rules atomic energy, sex, the Mafia, hidden resources, the stock market, obsessions, the subconscious, and the underworld.

Important Stuff to Know, III
Oils, Herbs, and Incence

Ashes	Ashes banish and dispel any and all influences.
Barley	Barley protects and keeps evil and negativity away.
Basil	Basil attracts money, love, good luck, and customers to your place of business. It repels evil and promotes fidelity in relationships.
Burdock	Burdock protects, promotes healing, and drives away evil and negativity.
Cattail	Cattails are used to induce lust.
Cedar	Cedar cleanses, protects, purifies, and creates a sacred space.
Chamomile	Chamomile calms things down. It can also be used in money and love spells.
Chili Peppers	Chili induces passion and lust. It spices up your sex life and breaks hexes.
Cinnamon	Cinnamon is used to attract love, wealth, and prosperity. It raises the vibrations to a high spiritual level and has a healing effect as well.
Clove	Clove insures total success in any matter and is used much like cinnamon. It makes you attractive to the opposite sex. Some people say it stops gossip.
Coffee	Coffee energizes, quickens, and speeds things up. It wakes the mind up to new ways of seeing things.

Comfrey	Comfrey is used to protect you while you're traveling. You can also use it to make your partner think of marriage.
Frankincense	Frankincense creates sacred space. It clears, protects, and brings the Spirit of God into any situation. It also heals, consecrates, and purifies everything. It's an excellent incense to use in any spell that involves spiritual growth work. If you can't find frankincense you can substitute rosemary.
Garlic	Garlic is used to dispel evil and bad vibes and drive out negativity.
Ginger	Ginger insures total success in any endeavor. It also attracts wealth and prosperity.
Iron	Anything made of iron protects you. Nails, iron spikes, horseshoes, and iron filings are used to protect and guard whatever you are doing.
Lavender	Lavender promotes peace and healing. It protects and creates an atmosphere of love and joy. In the old days, prostitutes wore lavender to attract customers to their business. This has caused it to be used in spells for love and lust as well.
Lemon	Lemons clear and drive away bad vibrations. They can be used in image magic in place of a poppet.
Mace	Mace insures that you will succeed at whatever you do. It also increases your psychic ability.
Marigolds	Marigolds are "solar" flowers and they attract respect and admiration. They also insure success and make all your dreams come true.
Morning Glory	Morning glory seeds dispel nightmares.
Musk	Musk empowers any spell and makes your intentions stronger. It is sexual and attractive. Musk is "male" and it functions to dominate and take control of situations. It induces lust. Musk also induces strength and courage and is good to use in any spell where you need an extra "kick."

Myrrh	Myrrh bestows peace and drives out evil and negativity. It raises the energy in any spell to a higher, more spiritual level.
Nutmeg	Nutmeg brings luck and is used to attract wealth and prosperity. It can be used in spells to insure fidelity also.
Onion	Onions absorb negative energy and are used to clear, protect, and keep away illness.
Orrisroot	Orrisroot binds, protects, and strengthens the effect of any spell. It draws love and is used in love spells as well.
Patchouli	Patchouli is an all-purpose scent. It can be used to banish *and* attract. It is sexual and used in spells to amplify that element. Patchouli is also used in money spells.
Pecans	Pecans are used in employment spells.
Peppermint	Peppermint is used to excite things and to dispel negativity.
Pine	Pine is used for success, protection, prosperity, wealth, long life, and health.
Rice	Rice is a symbol for abundance and fertility. It counteracts want and lack.
Rose	Rose is used in love spells. It encourages faithfulness, lasting ties, and peaceful, healing vibes. Rose is used to replace fear with unconditional love.
Rosemary	Rosemary protects, cleanses, and purifies. It strengthens the memory. Rosemary insures that in *any* male-female interaction that the female will hold the power. It can also be used in love spells.
Sage	Sage protects, cleanses, and creates a sacred space.
Sea Salt	Sea salt protects and insures that no other vibration will invade the space you are creating.
Wolf's Hair	Wolf's hair is the all-time *best* way to protect yourself from all evil.

Important Stuff to Know, IV
List of Spells, Charms, Herbal Remedies, and Other Useful Magic